The PLAYGROUND PROBLEM

Lauren
Scott Griffin

Illustrated by
Fred Folger

Esri Press
REDLANDS | CALIFORNIA

For Rowan

Esri Press, 380 New York Street, Redlands, California 92373-8100

Copyright © 2021 Esri

All rights reserved.

Printed in the United States of America

25 24 23 22 21   1 2 3 4 5 6 7 8 9 10

ISBN: 9781589485686

Library of Congress Control Number: 2020950566

For purchasing and distribution options (both domestic and international), please visit esripress.esri.com.

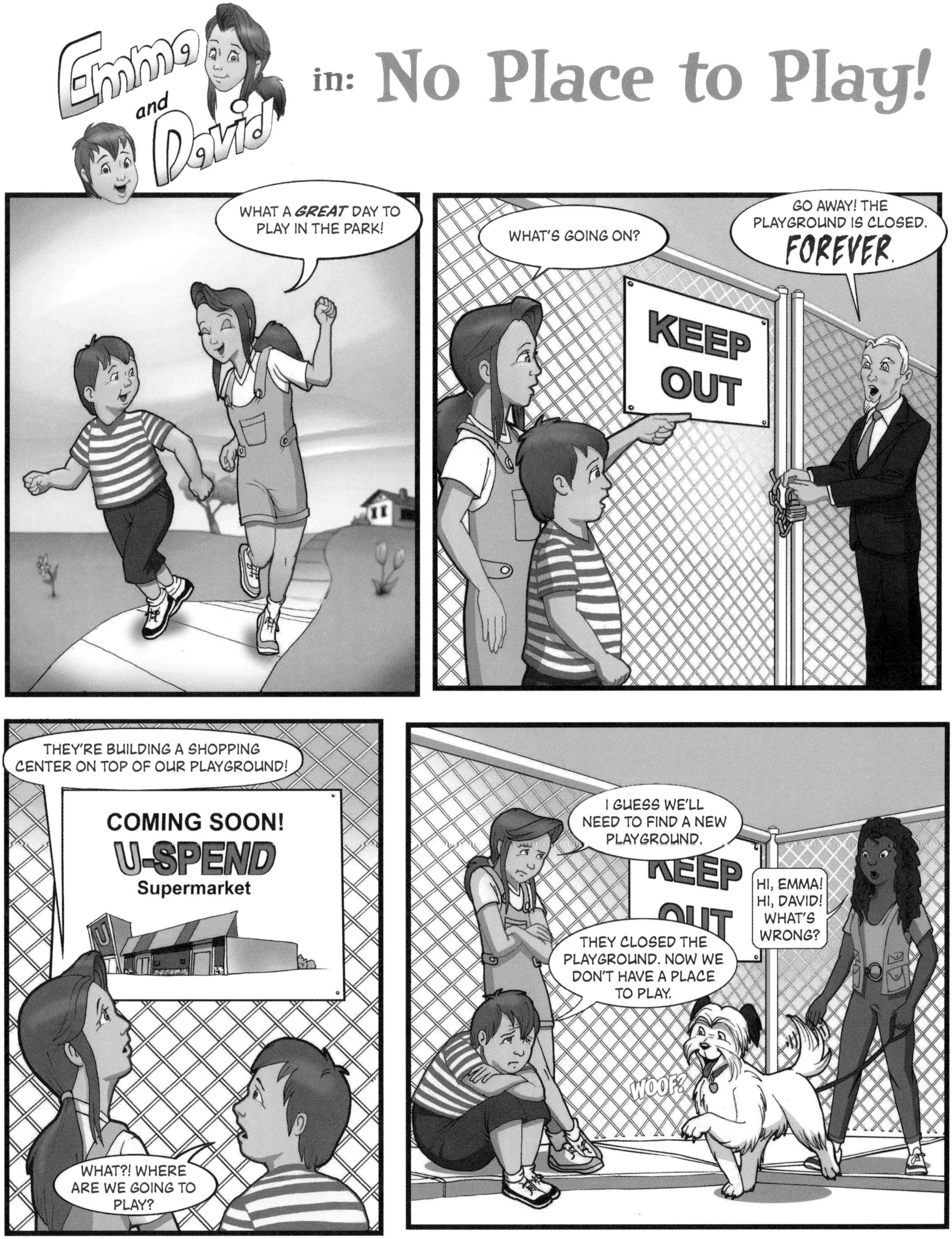
Emma and David
in: No Place to Play!
WHAT A GREAT DAY TO PLAY IN THE PARK!
WHAT'S GOING ON?
KEEP OUT
GO AWAY! THE PLAYGROUND IS CLOSED. FOREVER.
THEY'RE BUILDING A SHOPPING CENTER ON TOP OF OUR PLAYGROUND!
COMING SOON! U-SPEND Supermarket
WHAT?! WHERE ARE WE GOING TO PLAY?
I GUESS WE'LL NEED TO FIND A NEW PLAYGROUND.
HI, EMMA! HI, DAVID! WHAT'S WRONG?
THEY CLOSED THE PLAYGROUND. NOW WE DON'T HAVE A PLACE TO PLAY.
WOOF?

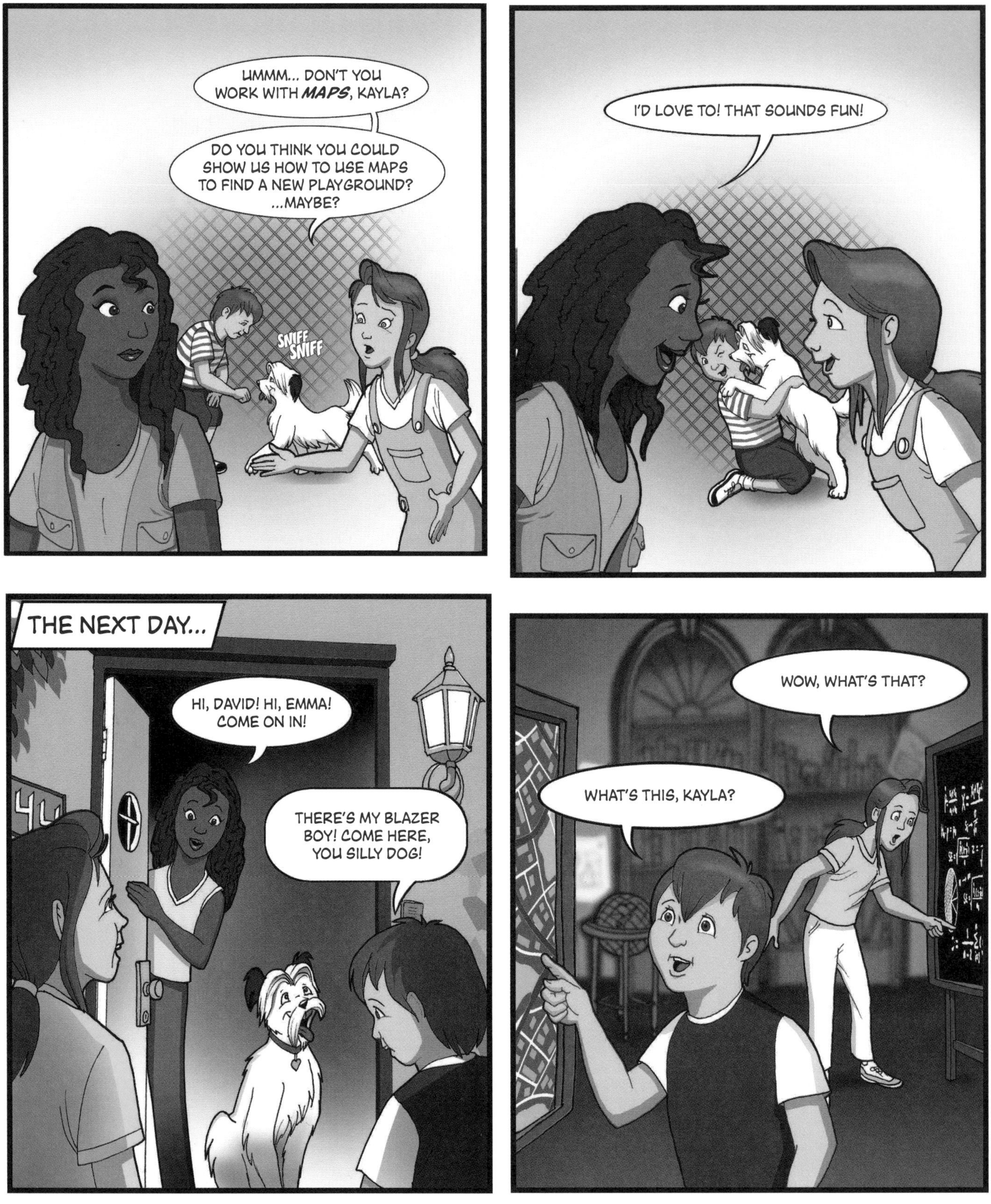

UMMM... DON'T YOU WORK WITH *MAPS*, KAYLA?
DO YOU THINK YOU COULD SHOW US HOW TO USE MAPS TO FIND A NEW PLAYGROUND? ...MAYBE?
SNIFF SNIFF
I'D LOVE TO! THAT SOUNDS FUN!
THE NEXT DAY...
HI, DAVID! HI, EMMA! COME ON IN!
THERE'S MY BLAZER BOY! COME HERE, YOU SILLY DOG!
WOW, WHAT'S THAT?
WHAT'S THIS, KAYLA?

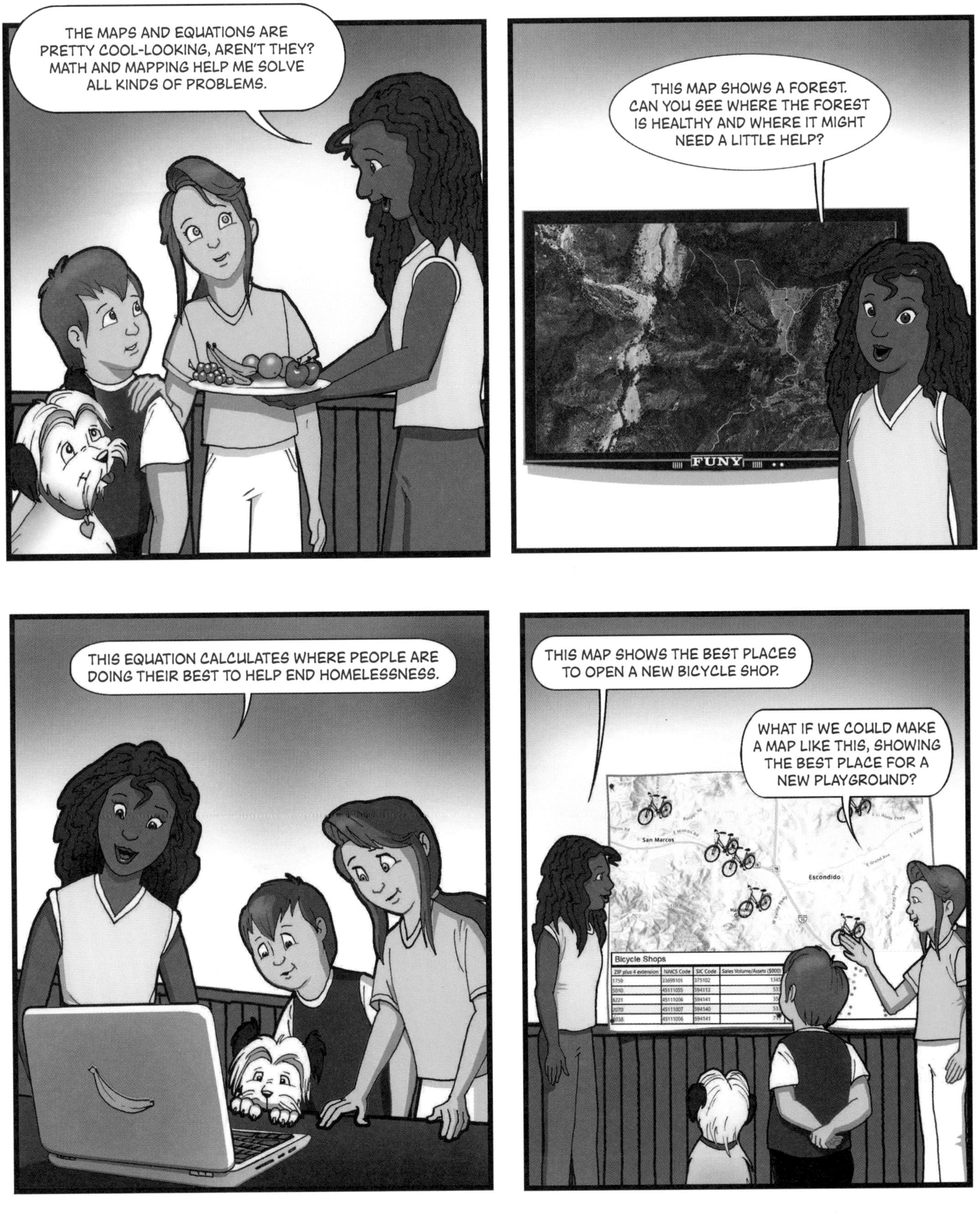
THE MAPS AND EQUATIONS ARE PRETTY COOL-LOOKING, AREN'T THEY? MATH AND MAPPING HELP ME SOLVE ALL KINDS OF PROBLEMS.
THIS MAP SHOWS A FOREST. CAN YOU SEE WHERE THE FOREST IS HEALTHY AND WHERE IT MIGHT NEED A LITTLE HELP?
FUNY
THIS EQUATION CALCULATES WHERE PEOPLE ARE DOING THEIR BEST TO HELP END HOMELESSNESS.
THIS MAP SHOWS THE BEST PLACES TO OPEN A NEW BICYCLE SHOP.
WHAT IF WE COULD MAKE A MAP LIKE THIS, SHOWING THE BEST PLACE FOR A NEW PLAYGROUND?
San Marcos
Escondido
Bicycle Shops

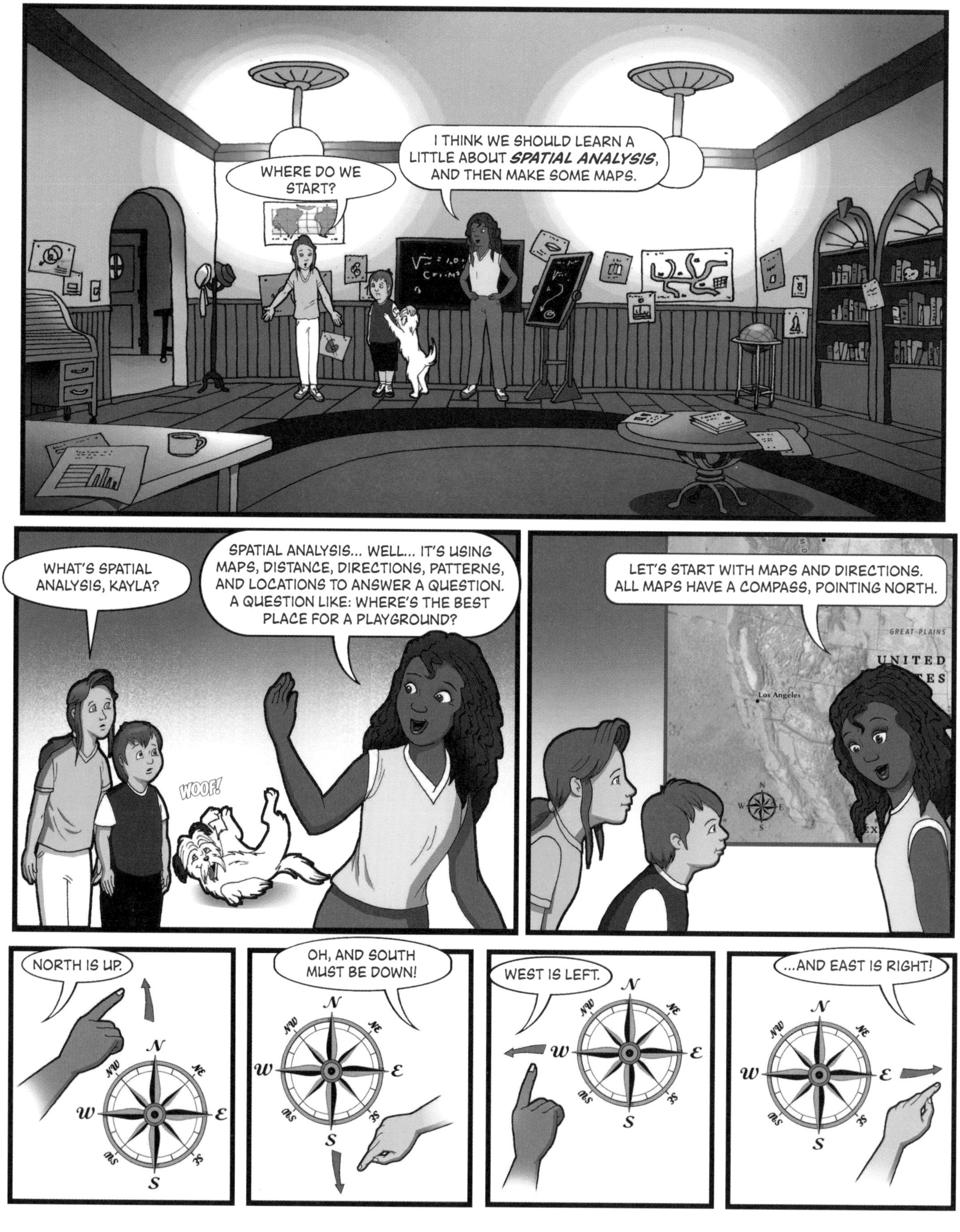
WHERE DO WE START?
I THINK WE SHOULD LEARN A LITTLE ABOUT *SPATIAL ANALYSIS*, AND THEN MAKE SOME MAPS.
WHAT'S SPATIAL ANALYSIS, KAYLA?
SPATIAL ANALYSIS... WELL... IT'S USING MAPS, DISTANCE, DIRECTIONS, PATTERNS, AND LOCATIONS TO ANSWER A QUESTION. A QUESTION LIKE: WHERE'S THE BEST PLACE FOR A PLAYGROUND?
WOOF!
LET'S START WITH MAPS AND DIRECTIONS. ALL MAPS HAVE A COMPASS, POINTING NORTH.
GREAT PLAINS
UNITED
Los Angeles
NORTH IS UP.
OH, AND SOUTH MUST BE DOWN!
WEST IS LEFT.
...AND EAST IS RIGHT!

Use compass directions to visit good places for a park while avoiding bad places. Draw your path as you go.

1. Beginning in the START HERE square, go north (N) one square, west (W) two squares, and north (N) one square.
2. Go northwest (NW) one square.
3. Go northeast (NE) two squares.
4. Go northwest (NW) one square and north (N) one square.

Check: You should be on the square with the snow-capped mountains.

5. Go southeast (SE) two squares and northeast (NE) two squares.
6. Go east (E) one square and southeast (SE) one square.
7. Go south (S) two squares and west (W) one square.
8. Go southeast (SE) one square.
9. Go south (S) two squares.
10. Go southwest (SW) one square and west (W) one square.
11. Go west (W) two squares and you're back where you started!

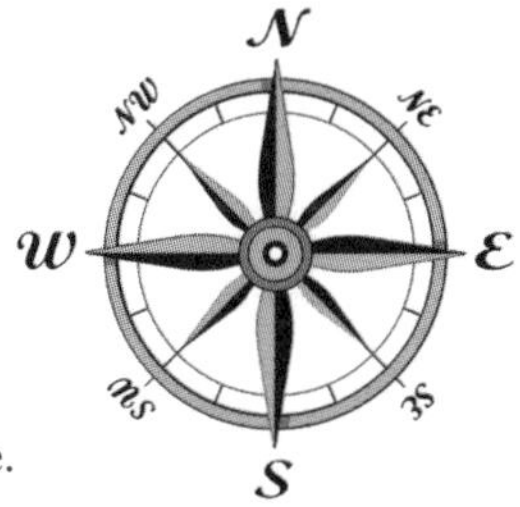
N
NE
E
SE
S
SW
W
NW

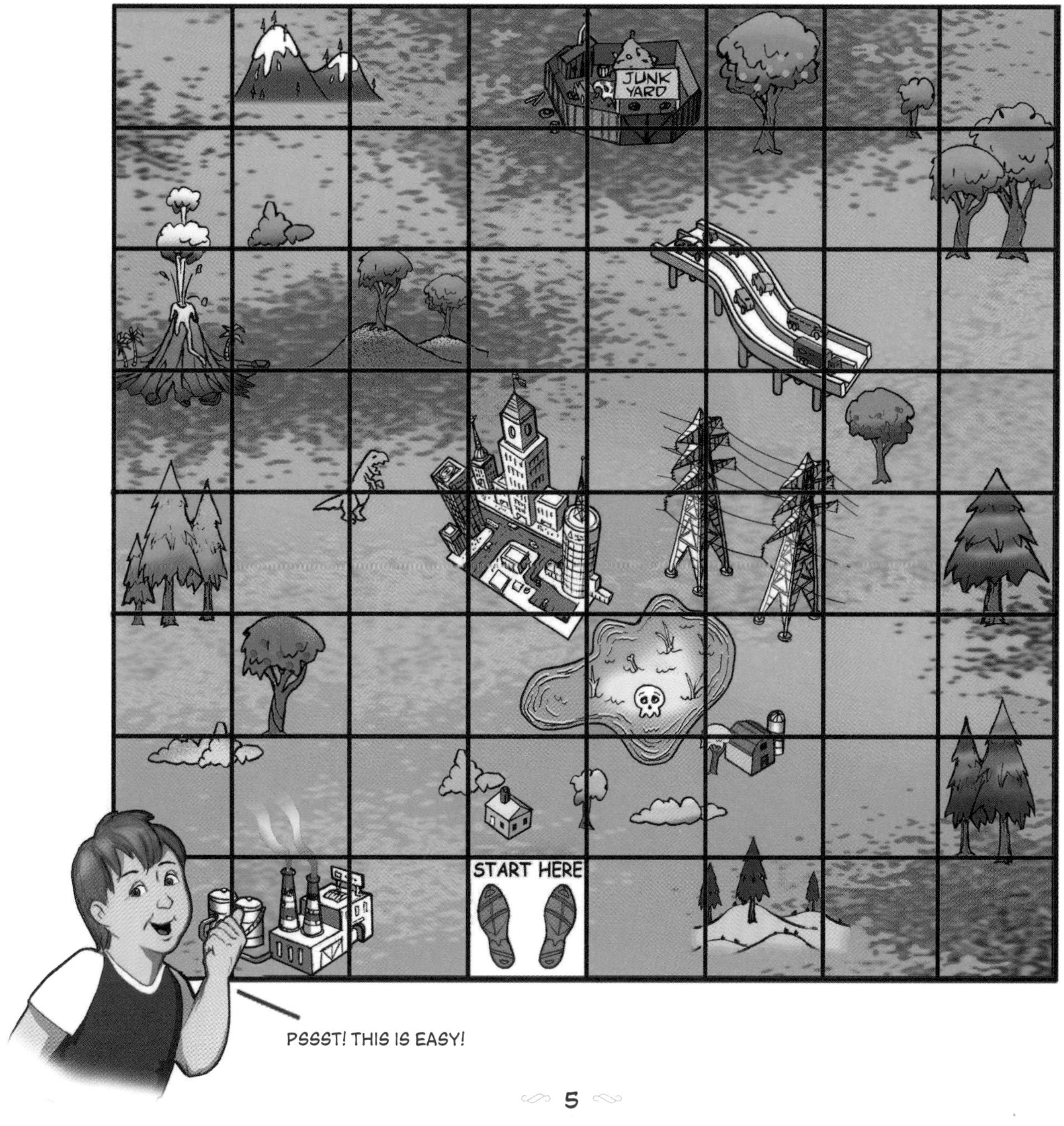
JUNK YARD
START HERE
PSSST! THIS IS EASY!

in: The Sun Compass

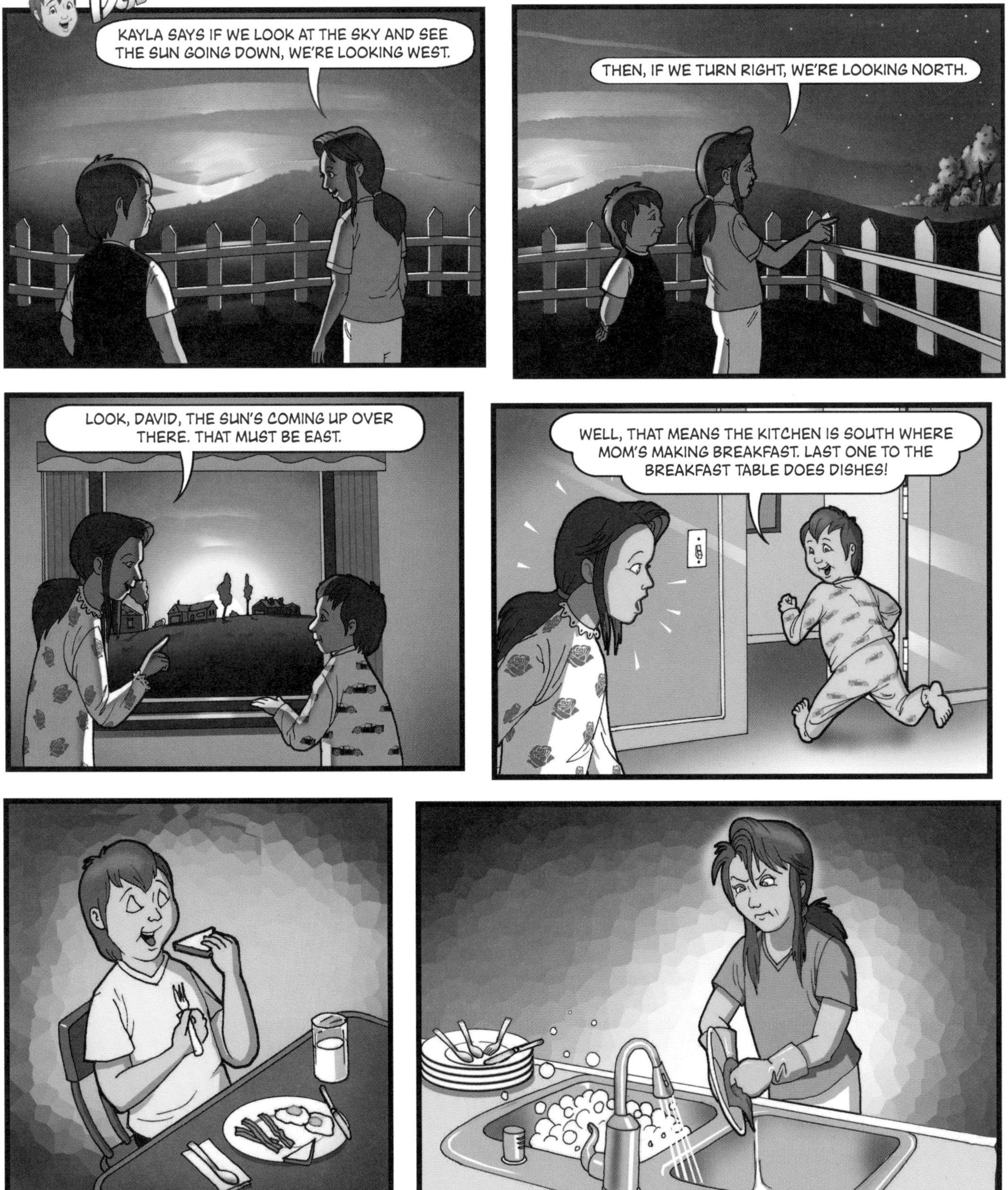

KAYLA SAYS IF WE LOOK AT THE SKY AND SEE THE SUN GOING DOWN, WE'RE LOOKING WEST.
THEN, IF WE TURN RIGHT, WE'RE LOOKING NORTH.
LOOK, DAVID, THE SUN'S COMING UP OVER THERE. THAT MUST BE EAST.
WELL, THAT MEANS THE KITCHEN IS SOUTH WHERE MOM'S MAKING BREAKFAST. LAST ONE TO THE BREAKFAST TABLE DOES DISHES!

Where is the best place for a new park?

The wind from the ocean blows the factory smoke to the east. Is it better to build the park somewhere west of the factory or somewhere east of the factory? Why?

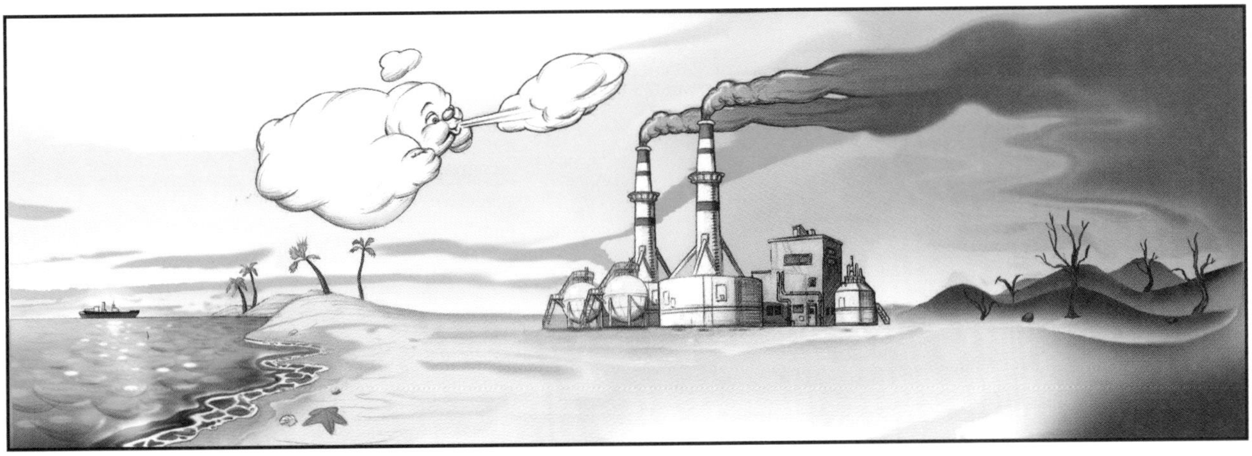

Should the park be closer to the busy freeway or closer to the quiet road? Why?

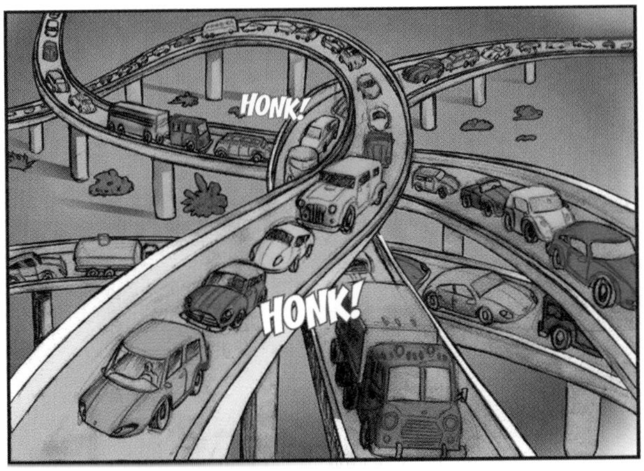
HONK!
HONK!

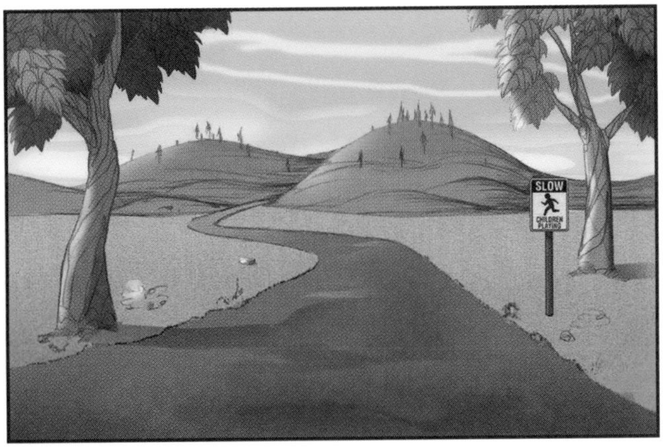
SLOW

Is it better if the park is close to where everyone lives, close to where everyone works, or far out in the country? Why?

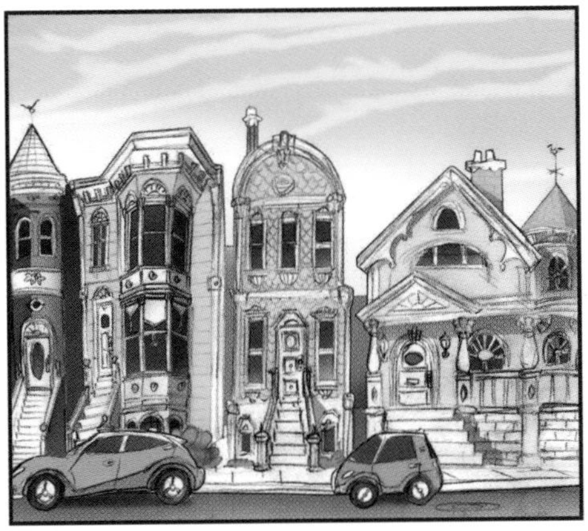

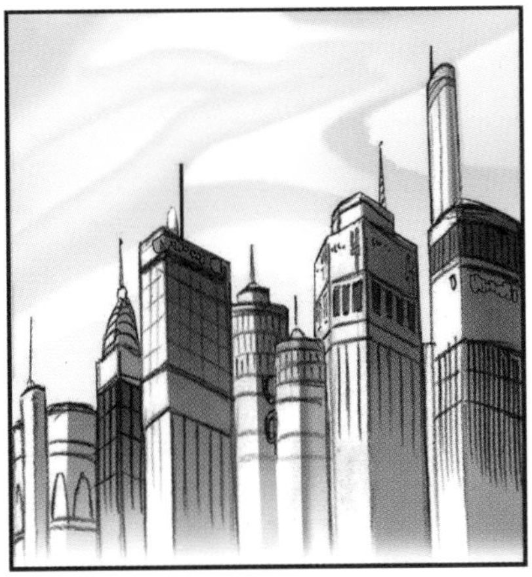

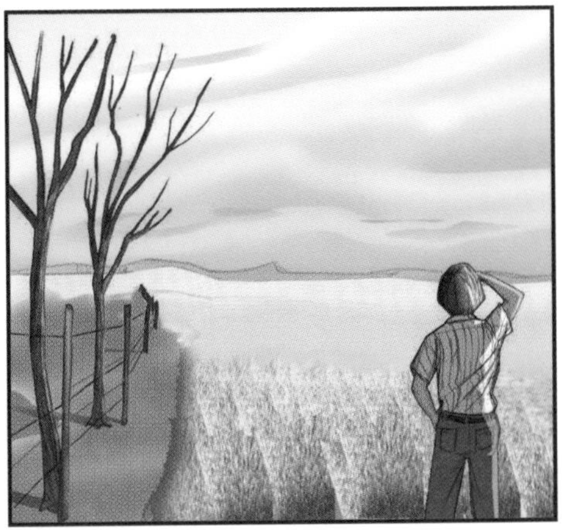

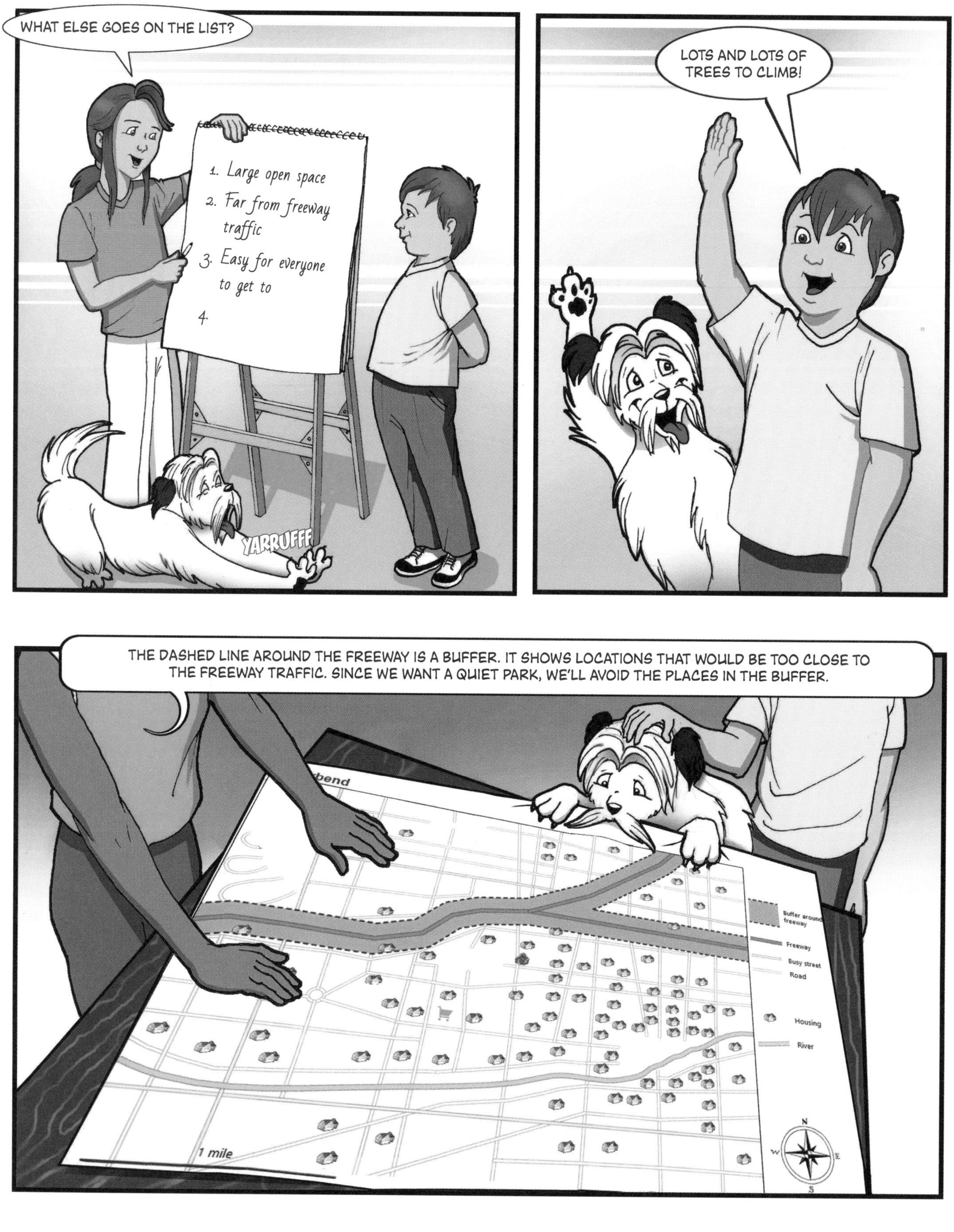

WHAT ELSE GOES ON THE LIST?
1. Large open space
2. Far from freeway traffic
3. Easy for everyone to get to
4.
YARRUFFF
LOTS AND LOTS OF TREES TO CLIMB!
THE DASHED LINE AROUND THE FREEWAY IS A BUFFER. IT SHOWS LOCATIONS THAT WOULD BE TOO CLOSE TO THE FREEWAY TRAFFIC. SINCE WE WANT A QUIET PARK, WE'LL AVOID THE PLACES IN THE BUFFER.
Buffer around freeway
Freeway
Busy street
Road
Housing
River
1 mile
N
W
E
S

Emma and David in: How Far Am I?

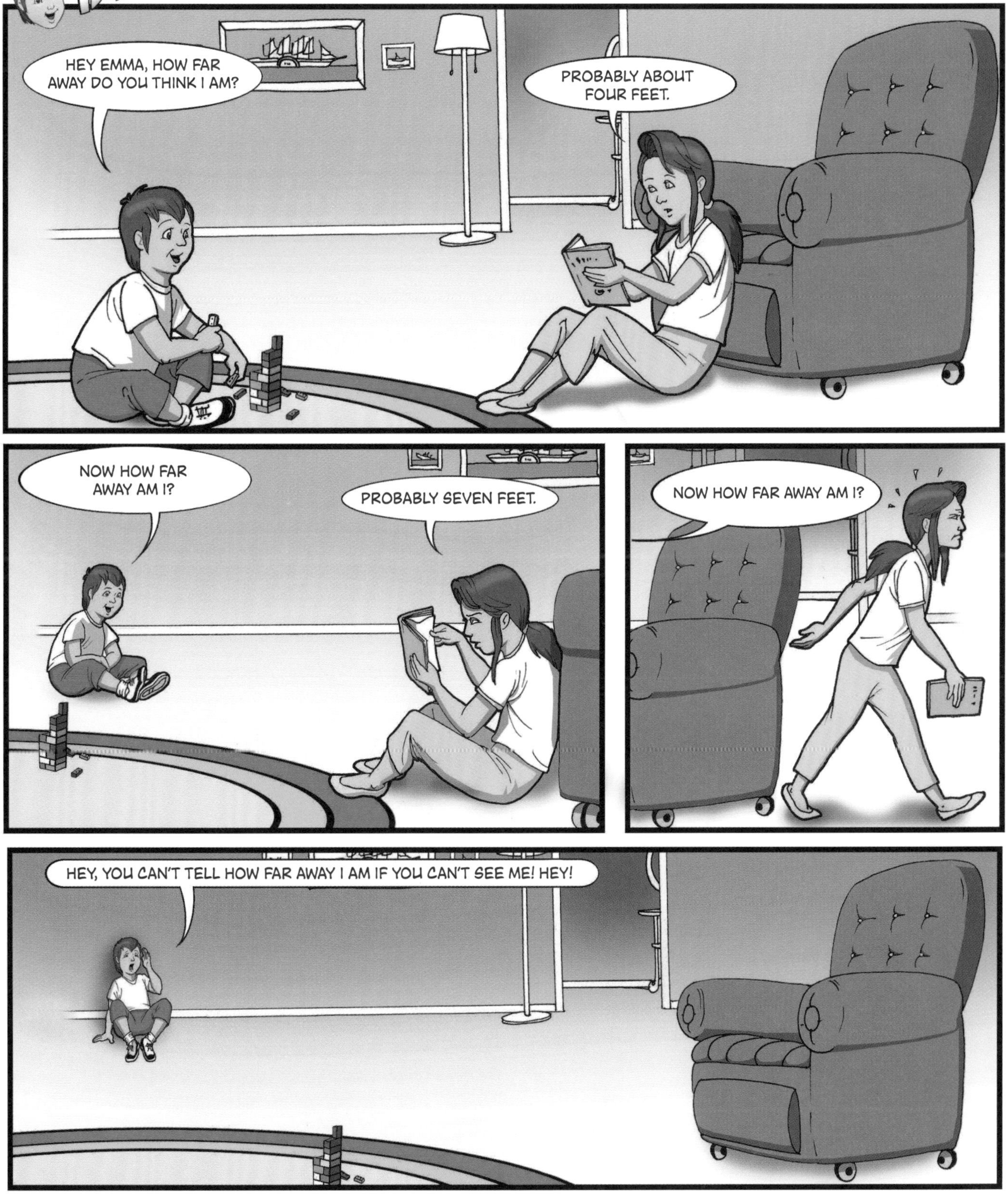
HEY EMMA, HOW FAR AWAY DO YOU THINK I AM?
PROBABLY ABOUT FOUR FEET.
NOW HOW FAR AWAY AM I?
PROBABLY SEVEN FEET.
NOW HOW FAR AWAY AM I?
HEY, YOU CAN'T TELL HOW FAR AWAY I AM IF YOU CAN'T SEE ME! HEY!

Maps show how far away things are

The kids are playing in the park. If the park is 10 minutes from the library, how far do you think the park is from the school?

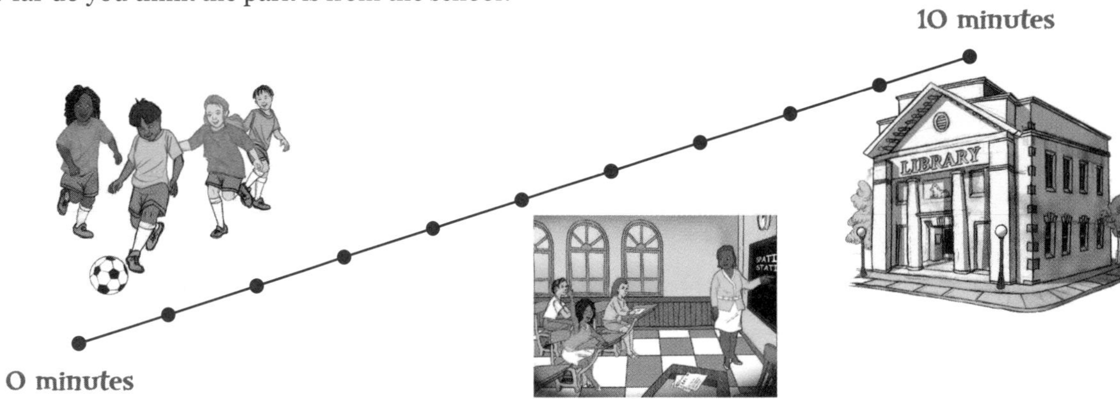
10 minutes
LIBRARY
0 minutes

If the store is 20 miles away from the bike shop at mile 0, do you think the park is 15 miles away from the bike shop or 5 miles away from the bike shop?

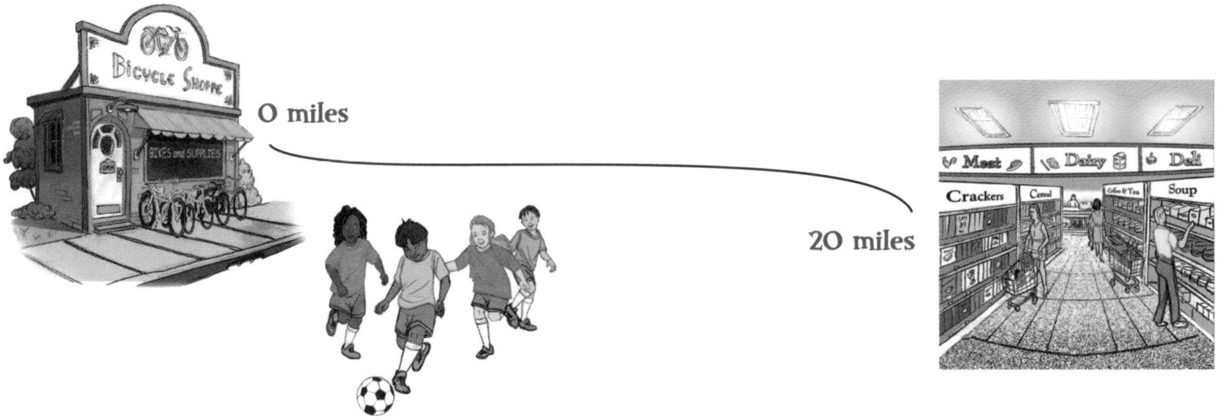
Bicycle Shoppe
BIKES and SUPPLIES
0 miles
Meat
Dairy
Deli
Crackers
Soup
20 miles

Which letter, **A**, **B**, or **C**, is closest to everything (the park, the school, and the store)?

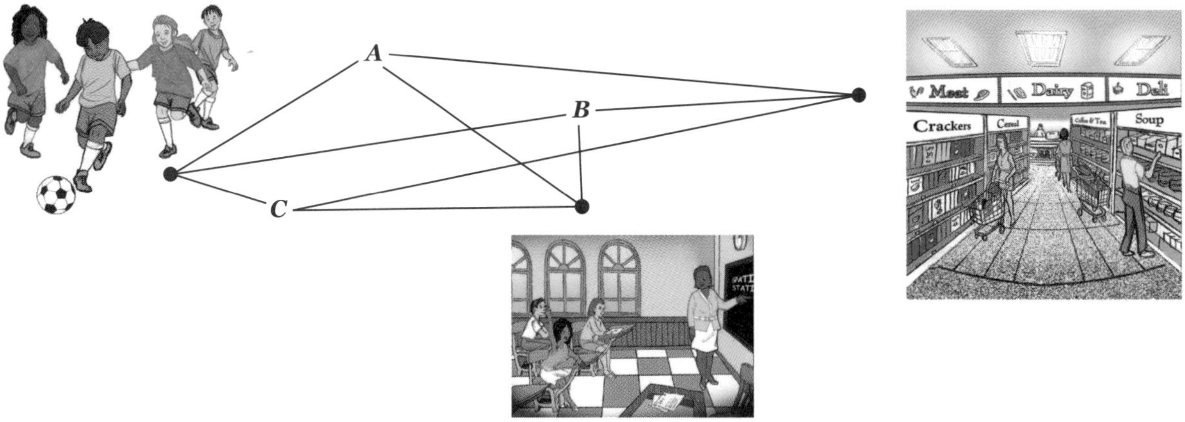
A
B
C
Meat
Dairy
Deli
Crackers
Soup

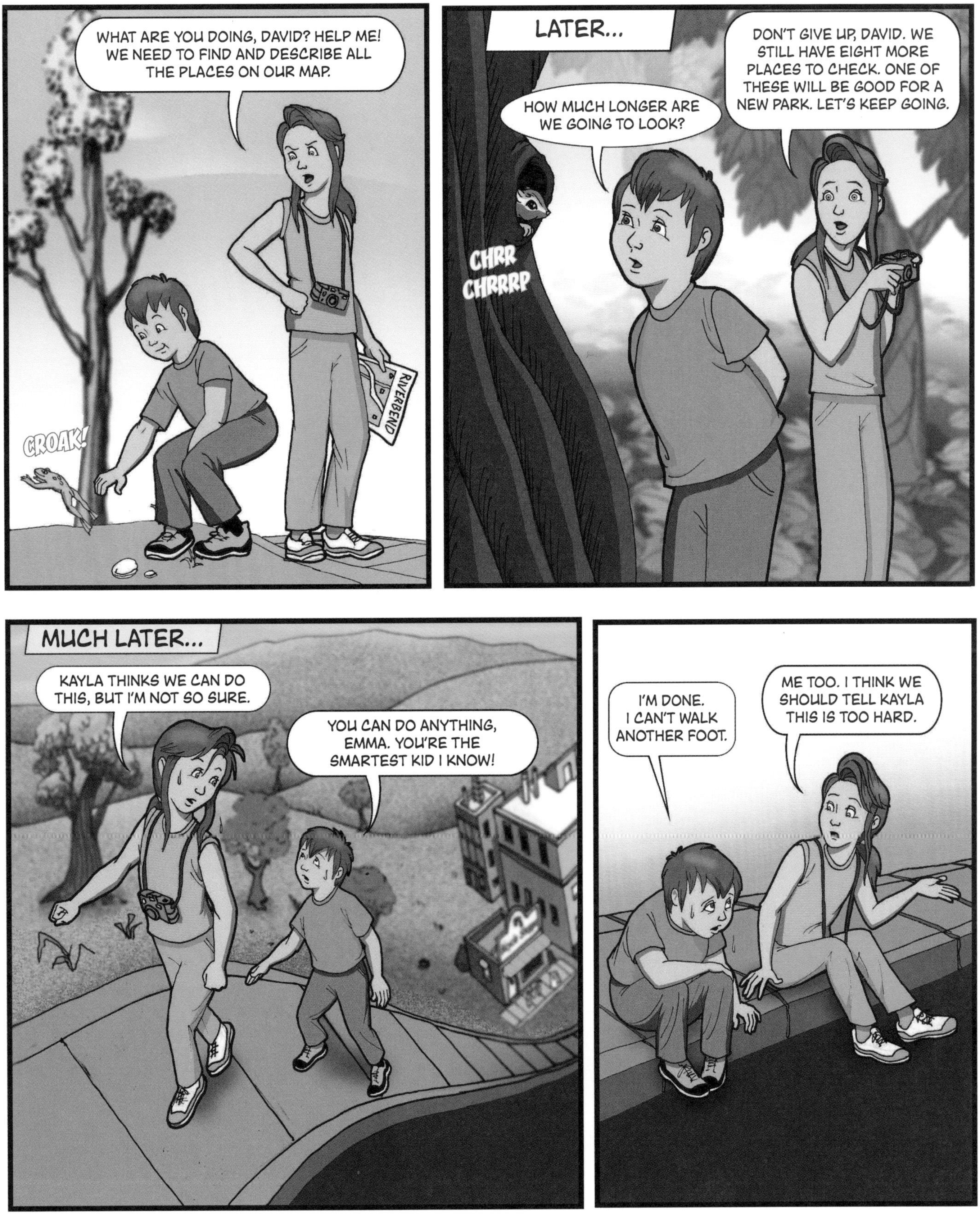
WHAT ARE YOU DOING, DAVID? HELP ME! WE NEED TO FIND AND DESCRIBE ALL THE PLACES ON OUR MAP.
RIVERBEND
CROAK!
LATER...
HOW MUCH LONGER ARE WE GOING TO LOOK?
DON'T GIVE UP, DAVID. WE STILL HAVE EIGHT MORE PLACES TO CHECK. ONE OF THESE WILL BE GOOD FOR A NEW PARK. LET'S KEEP GOING.
CHRR CHRRRP
MUCH LATER...
KAYLA THINKS WE CAN DO THIS, BUT I'M NOT SO SURE.
YOU CAN DO ANYTHING, EMMA. YOU'RE THE SMARTEST KID I KNOW!
I'M DONE. I CAN'T WALK ANOTHER FOOT.
ME TOO. I THINK WE SHOULD TELL KAYLA THIS IS TOO HARD.

Choose the best park locations

Emma, David, Kayla, and Blazer have looked at lots of places around town. Below are the pictures they've taken. **Circle** each one that would be a good location for a park and mark an **X** on the places that would not be good for a park.

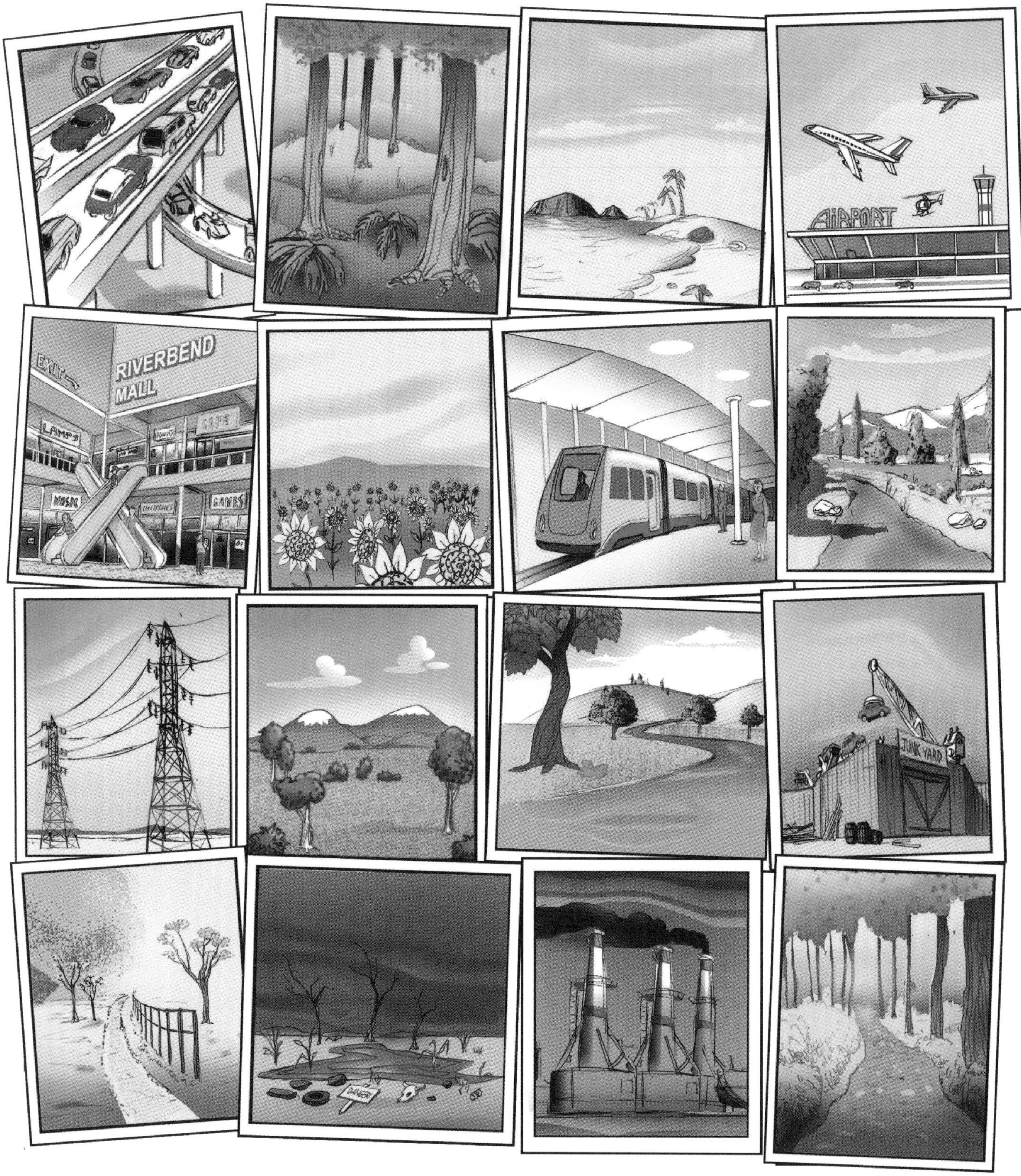
AIRPORT
EXIT
RIVERBEND MALL
LAMPS
CAFE
MUSIC
ELECTRONICS
GAMES
JUNK YARD
DANGER

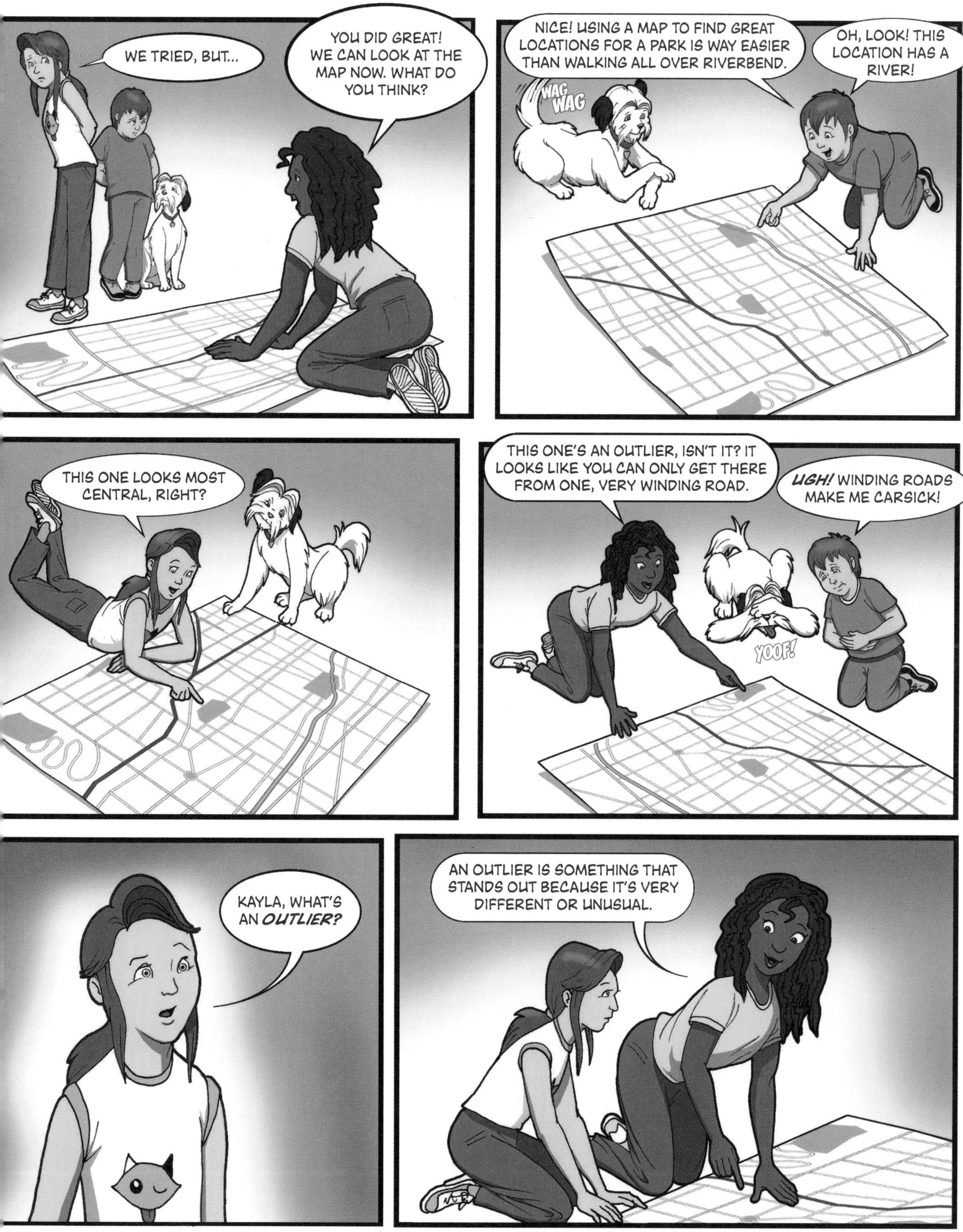
WE TRIED, BUT...
YOU DID GREAT! WE CAN LOOK AT THE MAP NOW. WHAT DO YOU THINK?
NICE! USING A MAP TO FIND GREAT LOCATIONS FOR A PARK IS WAY EASIER THAN WALKING ALL OVER RIVERBEND.
WAG WAG
OH, LOOK! THIS LOCATION HAS A RIVER!
THIS ONE LOOKS MOST CENTRAL, RIGHT?
THIS ONE'S AN OUTLIER, ISN'T IT? IT LOOKS LIKE YOU CAN ONLY GET THERE FROM ONE, VERY WINDING ROAD.
UGH! WINDING ROADS MAKE ME CARSICK!
YOOF!
KAYLA, WHAT'S AN OUTLIER?
AN OUTLIER IS SOMETHING THAT STANDS OUT BECAUSE IT'S VERY DIFFERENT OR UNUSUAL.

Identify outliers

Which person is the outlier?

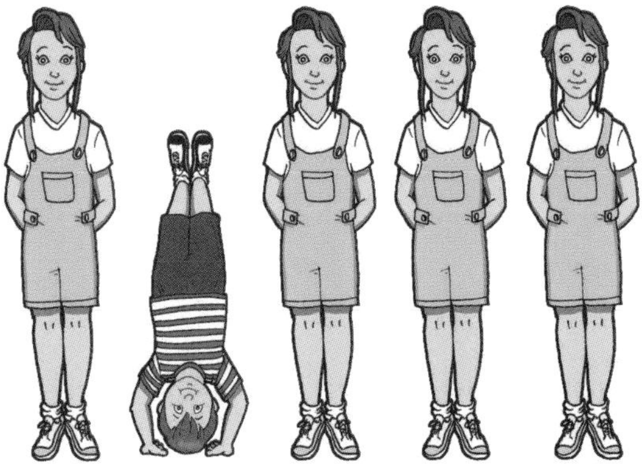

Which picture below has an outlier? What is it? Why is it an outlier?

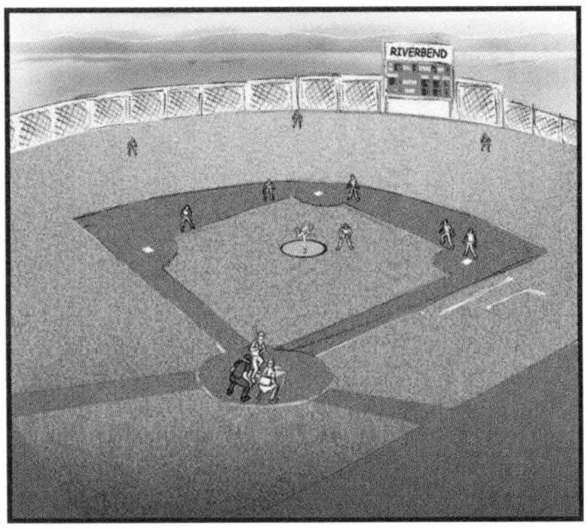
RIVERBEND

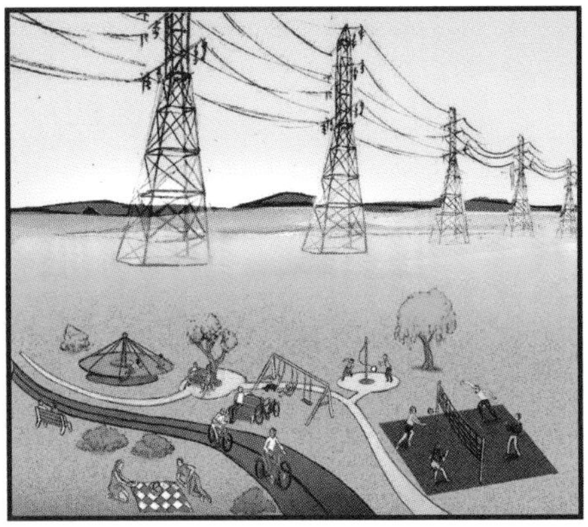

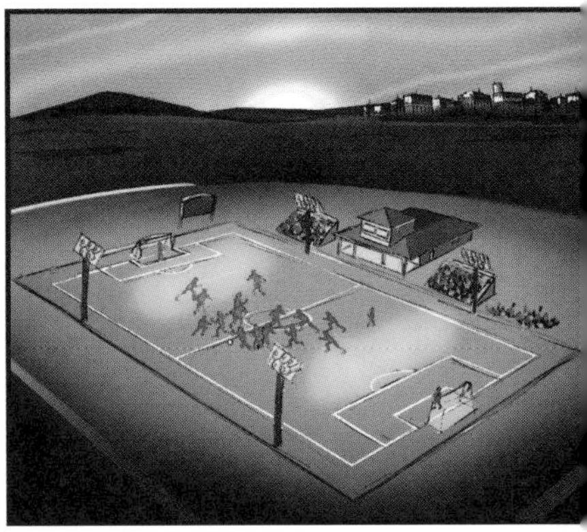

Can you spot five differences between these two pictures?

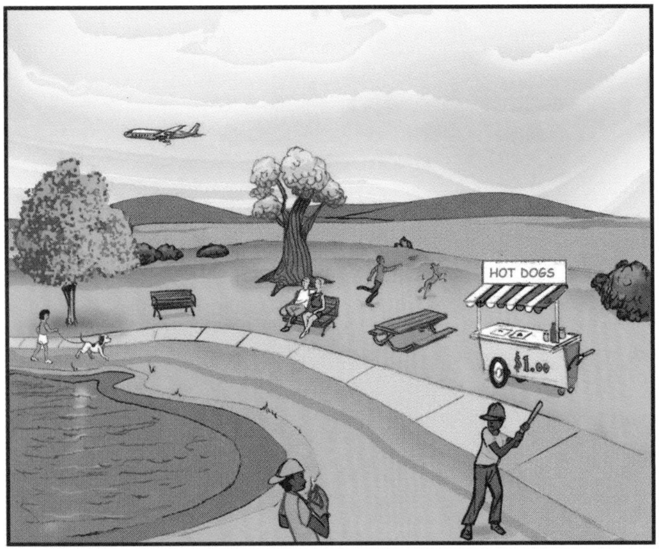
HOT DOGS
$1.00

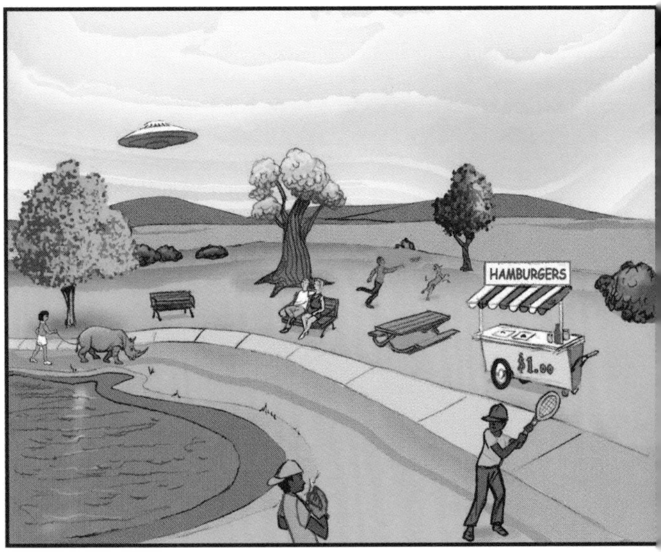
HAMBURGERS
$1.00

Emma and David in: Looking for Outliers

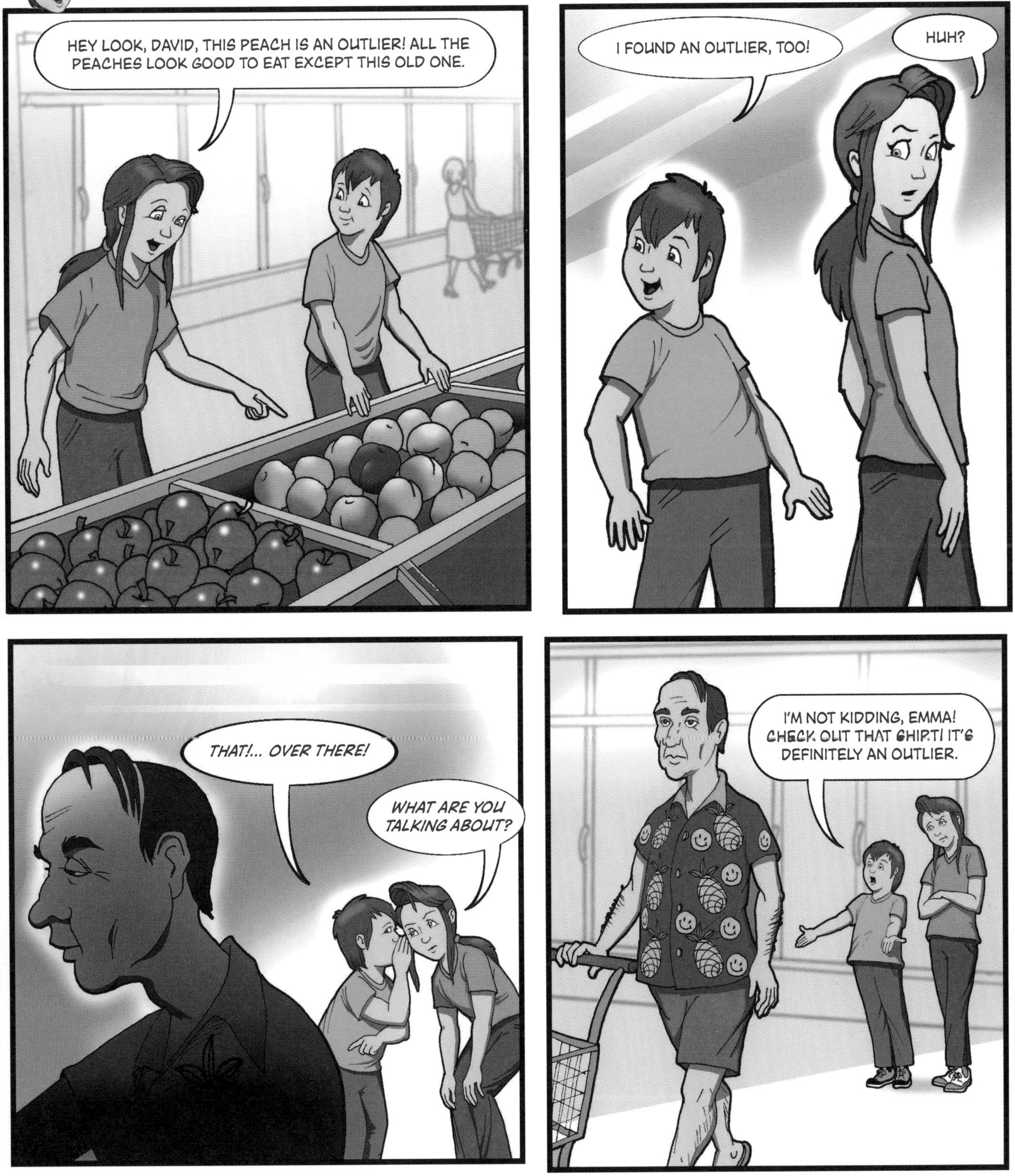
HEY LOOK, DAVID, THIS PEACH IS AN OUTLIER! ALL THE PEACHES LOOK GOOD TO EAT EXCEPT THIS OLD ONE.
I FOUND AN OUTLIER, TOO!
HUH?
THAT!... OVER THERE!
WHAT ARE YOU TALKING ABOUT?
I'M NOT KIDDING, EMMA! CHECK OUT THAT SHIRT! IT'S DEFINITELY AN OUTLIER.

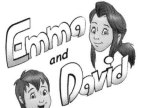

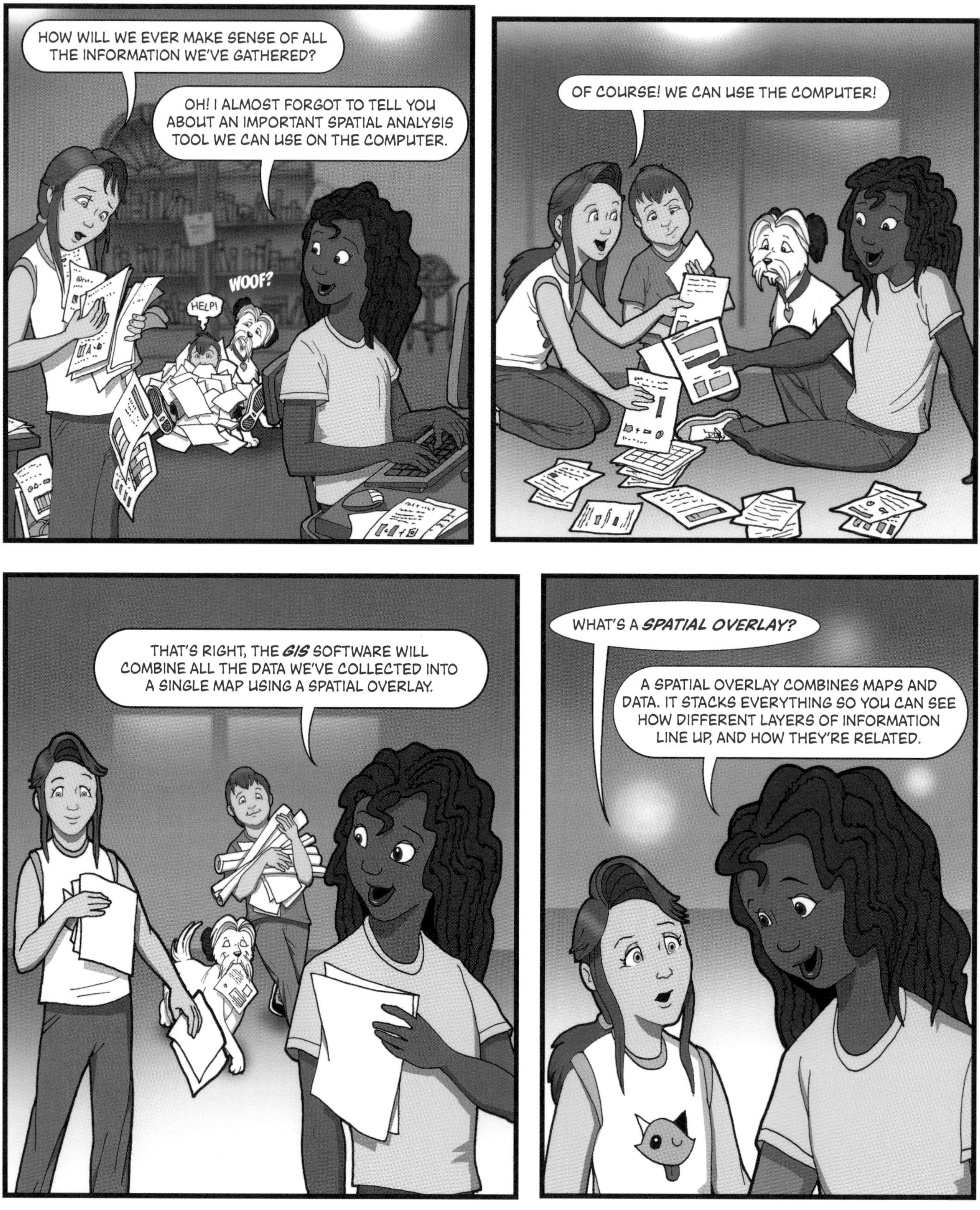
HOW WILL WE EVER MAKE SENSE OF ALL THE INFORMATION WE'VE GATHERED?
OH! I ALMOST FORGOT TO TELL YOU ABOUT AN IMPORTANT SPATIAL ANALYSIS TOOL WE CAN USE ON THE COMPUTER.
HELP!
WOOF?
OF COURSE! WE CAN USE THE COMPUTER!
THAT'S RIGHT, THE GIS SOFTWARE WILL COMBINE ALL THE DATA WE'VE COLLECTED INTO A SINGLE MAP USING A SPATIAL OVERLAY.
WHAT'S A SPATIAL OVERLAY?
A SPATIAL OVERLAY COMBINES MAPS AND DATA. IT STACKS EVERYTHING SO YOU CAN SEE HOW DIFFERENT LAYERS OF INFORMATION LINE UP, AND HOW THEY'RE RELATED.

Starting with spatial overlays

The coloring activities on the following pages show you how a spatial overlay works. The numbers on this map tell you how many people live in each square. Use the map legend to color each square according to which neighborhoods have no people (**white**), a few people (**light pink**), some people (**dark pink**), and many people (**red**).

Riverbend

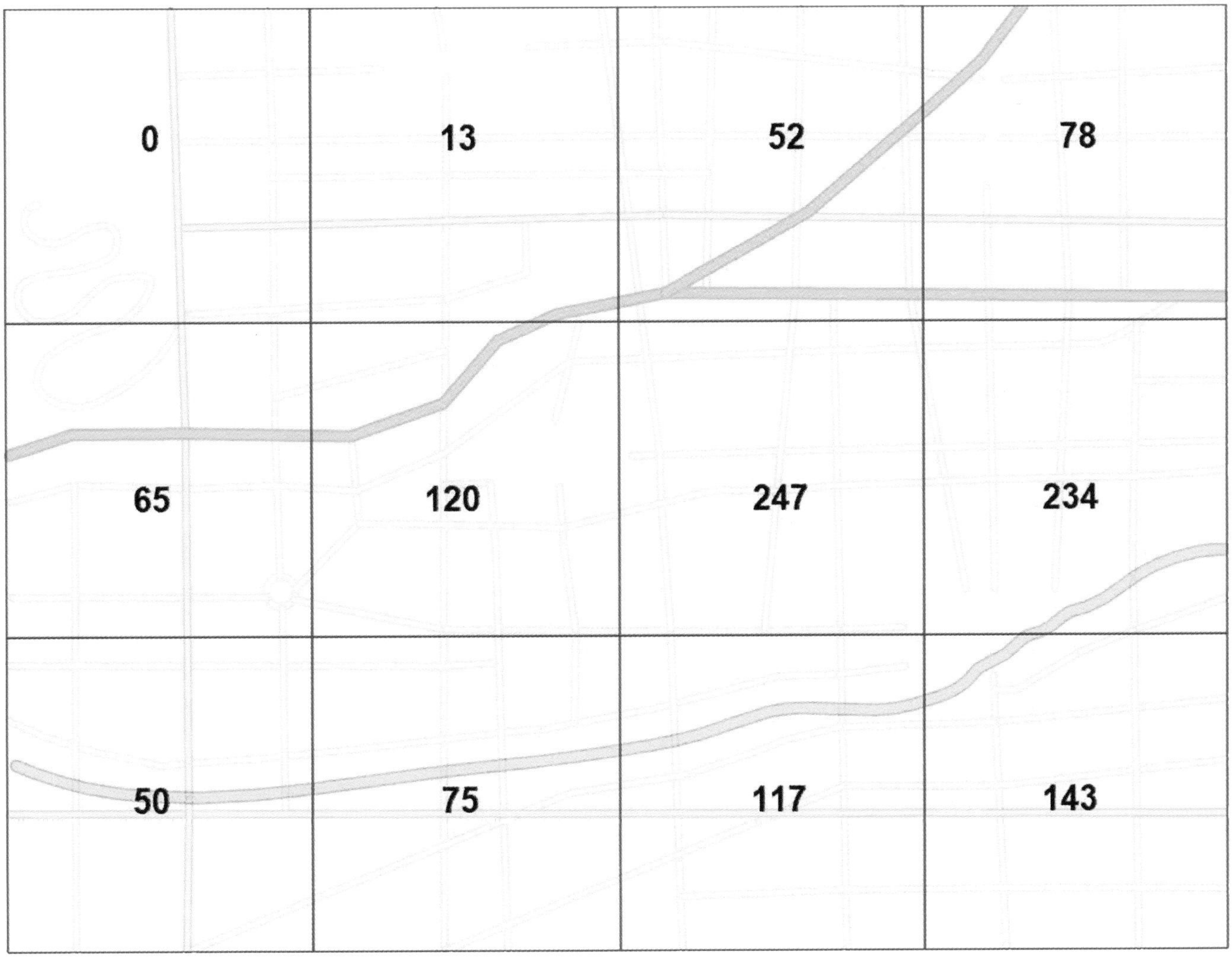

0
13
52
78
65
120
247
234
50
75
117
143

Legend

Number of people in each neighborhood

River

No people	A few people	Some people	Many people
0 people	From 1 to 100 people	From 101 to 200 people	More than 200 people

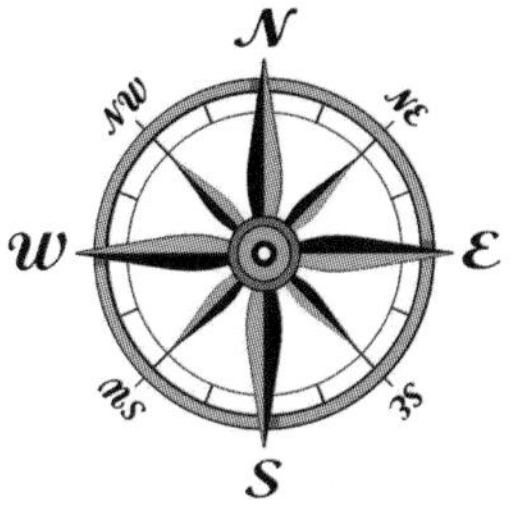

N
NW
NE
W
E
SW
SE
S

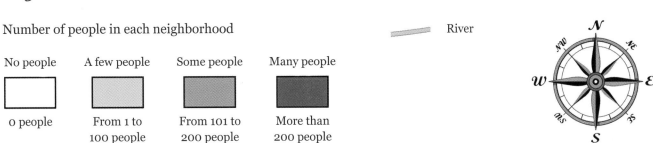

Avoid the freeway

You don't want the park to be too close to the freeway. Color the freeway **black**. Color the buffer around the freeway **gray**.

Riverbend

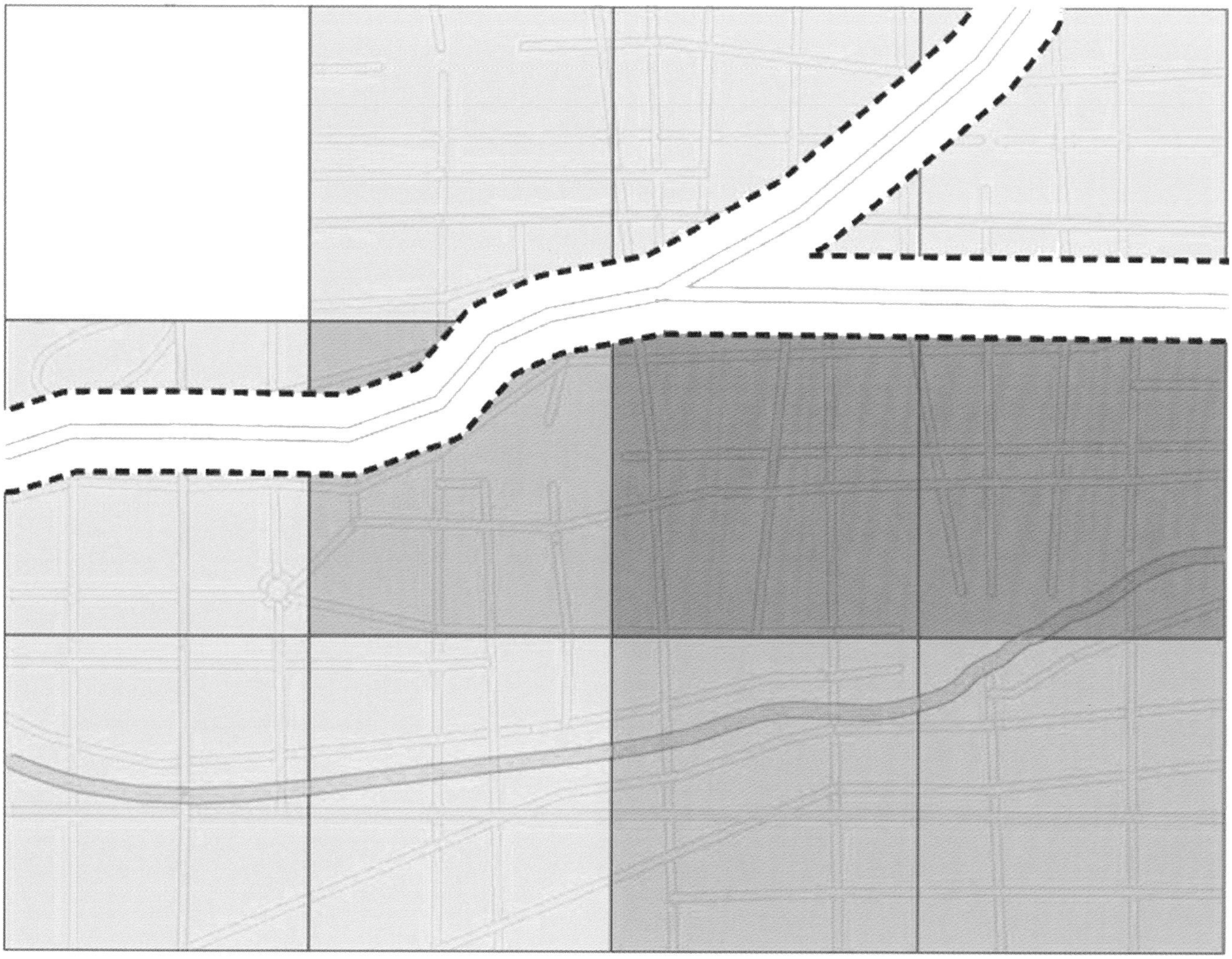

Legend

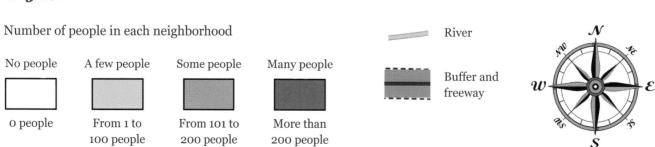

Number of people in each neighborhood

No people	A few people	Some people	Many people
0 people	From 1 to 100 people	From 101 to 200 people	More than 200 people

River

Buffer and freeway

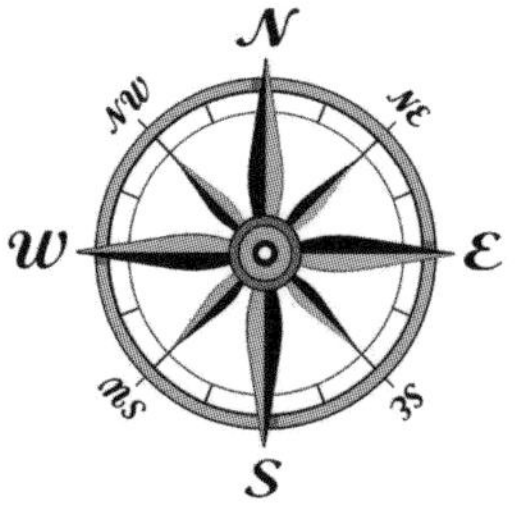
N
NE
E
SE
S
SW
W
NW

Narrow down the locations

The possible park locations have been added to your map. One park location is **too close to the freeway**. Cross it out. Cross out the park location in the corner where **there aren't any people and the road is winding**. Cross out the **two smallest park locations** where there are only a few people. You should have two park locations left.

Riverbend

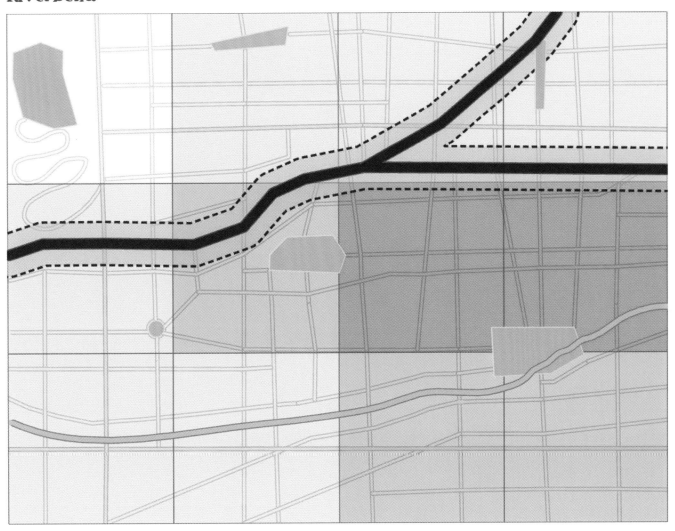

Legend

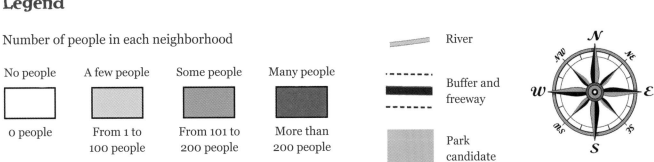

Number of people in each neighborhood

No people	A few people	Some people	Many people
0 people	From 1 to 100 people	From 101 to 200 people	More than 200 people

River

Buffer and freeway

Park candidate

Have fun coloring this page!

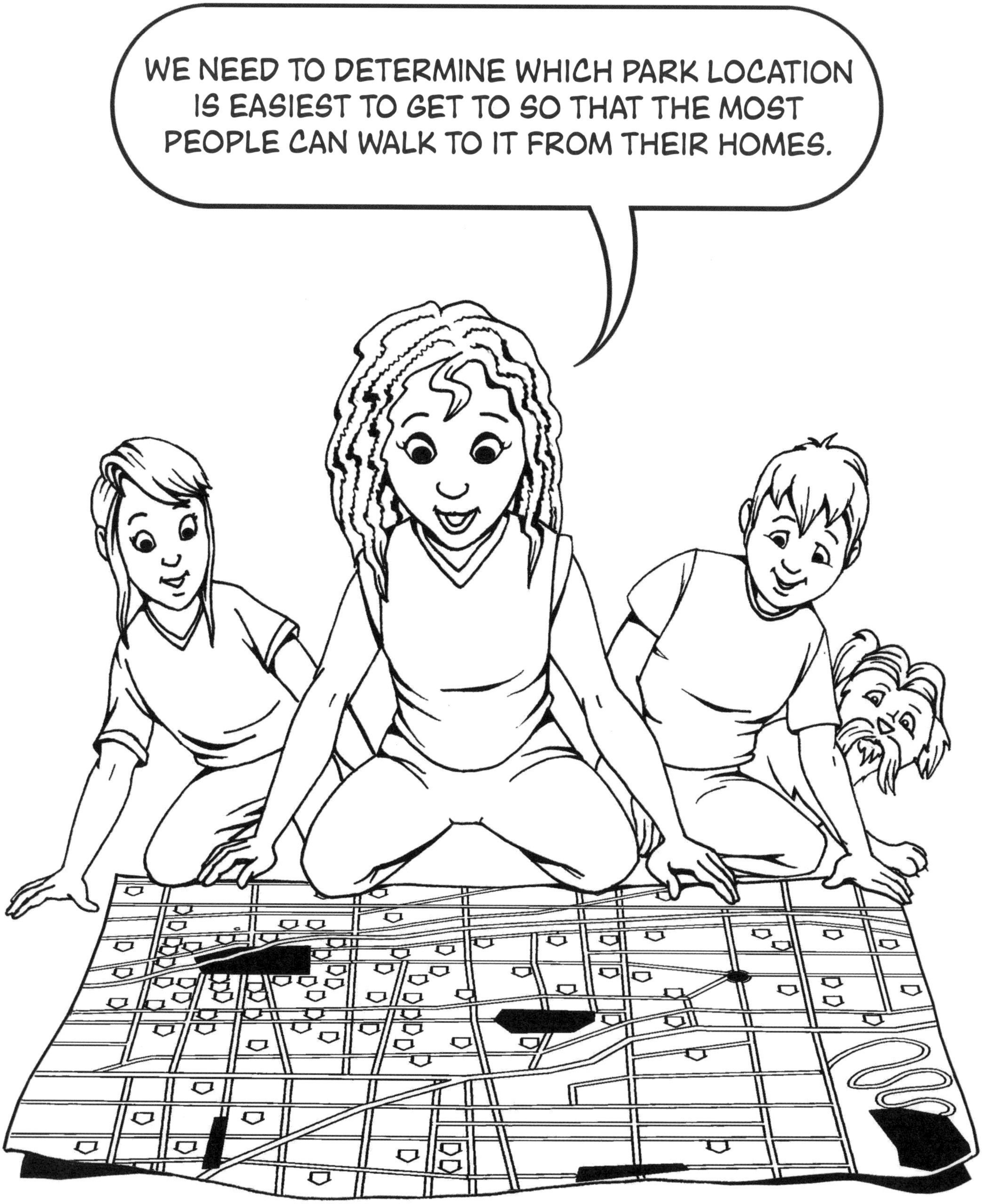
WE NEED TO DETERMINE WHICH PARK LOCATION IS EASIEST TO GET TO SO THAT THE MOST PEOPLE CAN WALK TO IT FROM THEIR HOMES.

Connect the dots to find who is close

Connect the dots to create a 10-minute walking distance buffer around each candidate park location. Everyone inside the buffer will be able to walk to the park in 10 minutes or less.

Riverbend

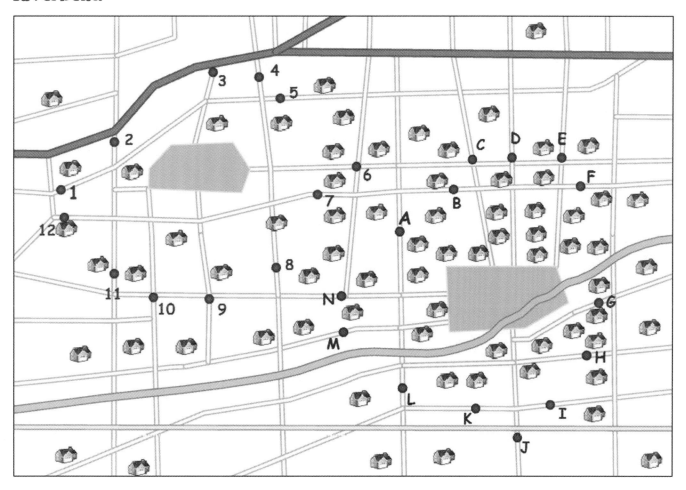

1
2
3
4
5
6
7
8
9
10
11
12
A
B
C
D
E
F
G
H
I
J
K
L
M
N

Legend

Freeway

Busy road

Street

River

Park candidate

Housing

N
NE
E
SE
S
SW
W
NW

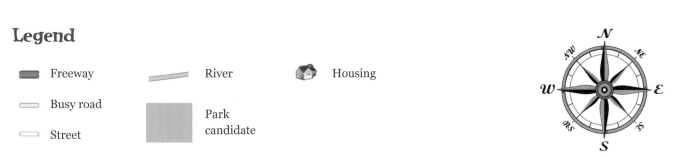

After you connect the dots, **which park has the most housing** inside the 10-minute walk time buffer?

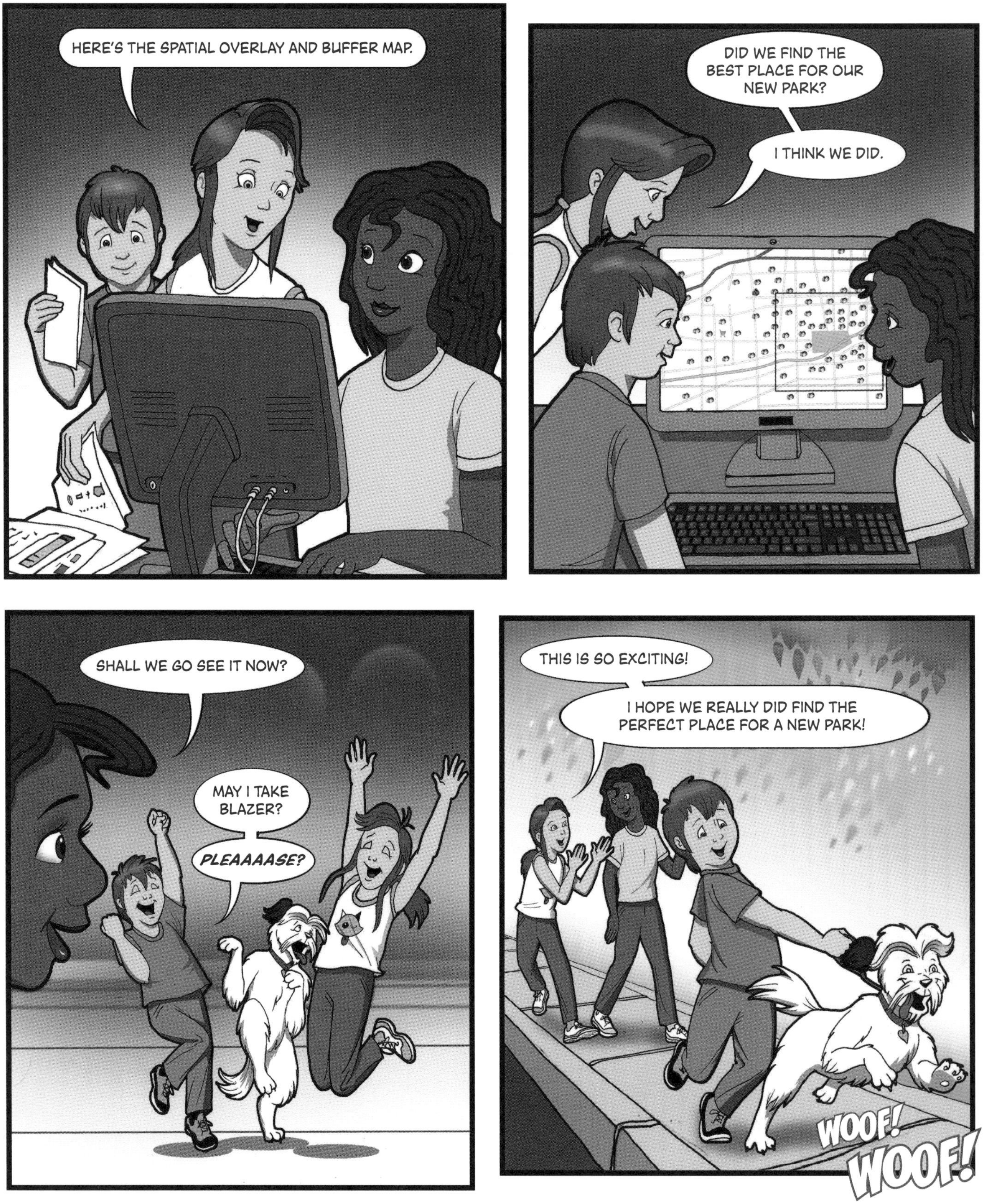
HERE'S THE SPATIAL OVERLAY AND BUFFER MAP.
DID WE FIND THE BEST PLACE FOR OUR NEW PARK?
I THINK WE DID.
SHALL WE GO SEE IT NOW?
MAY I TAKE BLAZER?
PLEAAAASE?
THIS IS SO EXCITING!
I HOPE WE REALLY DID FIND THE PERFECT PLACE FOR A NEW PARK!
WOOF! WOOF!

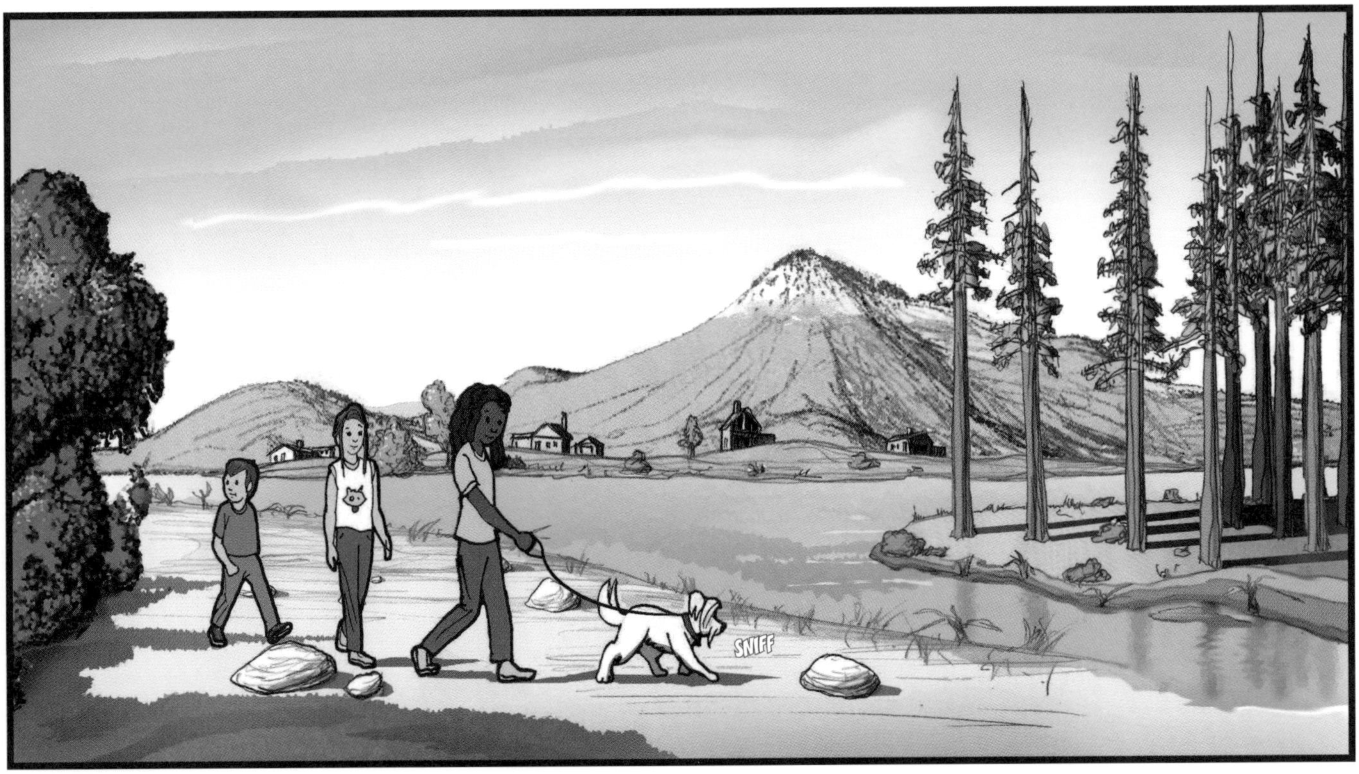
SNIFF

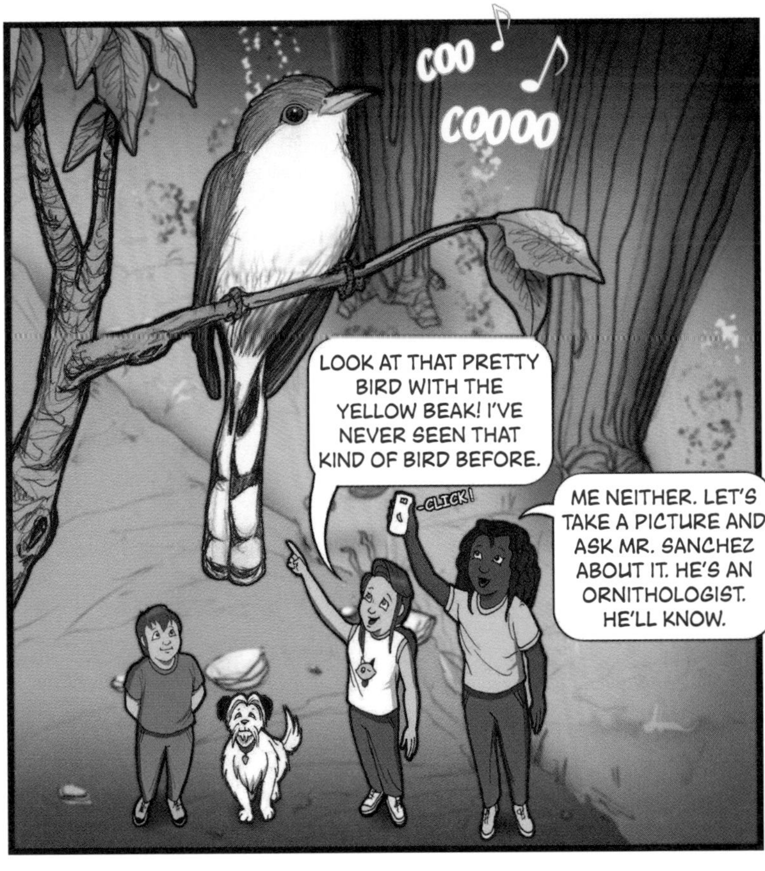
COO
COOOO
LOOK AT THAT PRETTY BIRD WITH THE YELLOW BEAK! I'VE NEVER SEEN THAT KIND OF BIRD BEFORE.
CLICK!
ME NEITHER. LET'S TAKE A PICTURE AND ASK MR. SANCHEZ ABOUT IT. HE'S AN ORNITHOLOGIST. HE'LL KNOW.

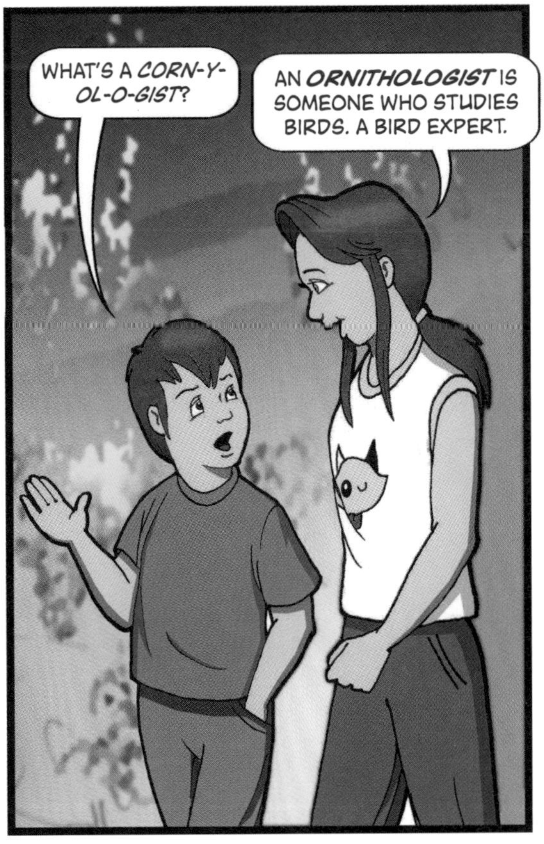
WHAT'S A *CORN-Y-OL-O-GIST*?
AN ***ORNITHOLOGIST*** IS SOMEONE WHO STUDIES BIRDS. A BIRD EXPERT.

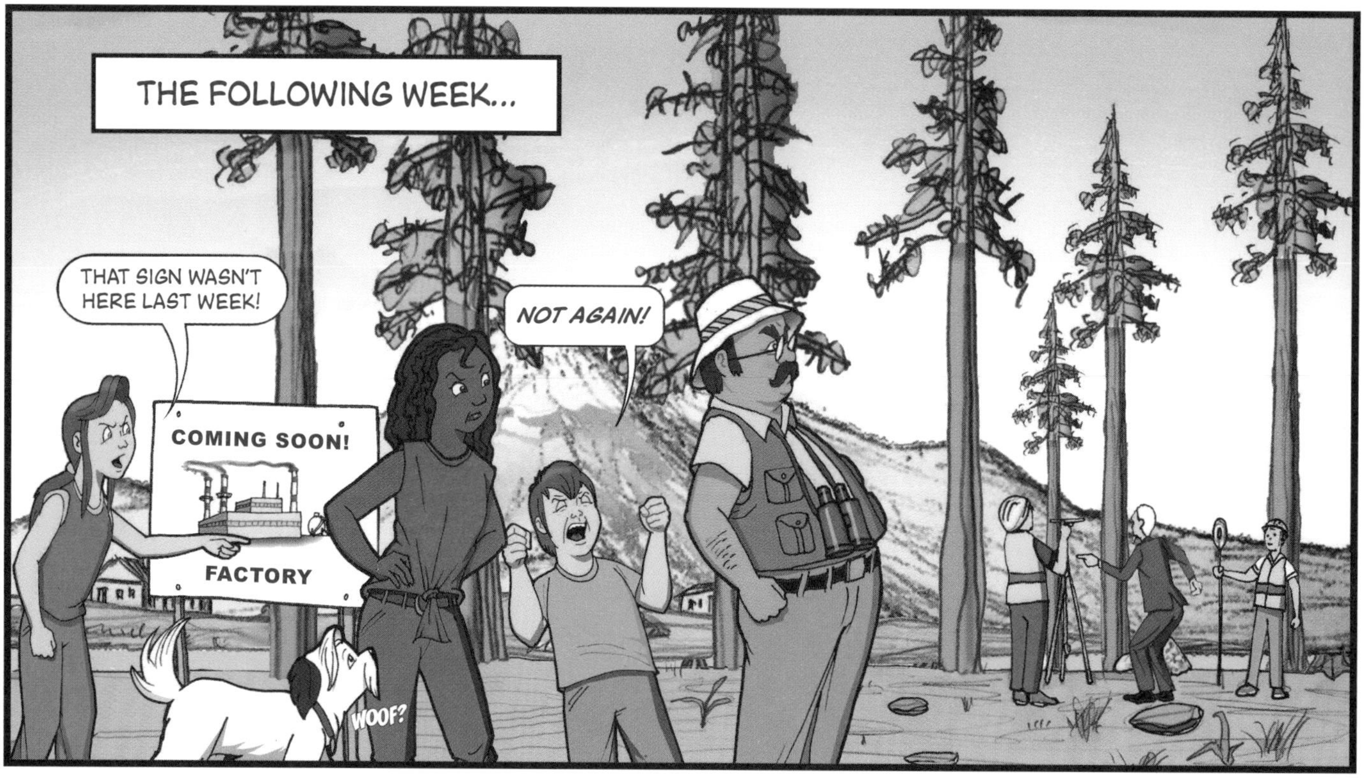
THE FOLLOWING WEEK...
THAT SIGN WASN'T HERE LAST WEEK!
COMING SOON!
FACTORY
NOT AGAIN!
WOOF?

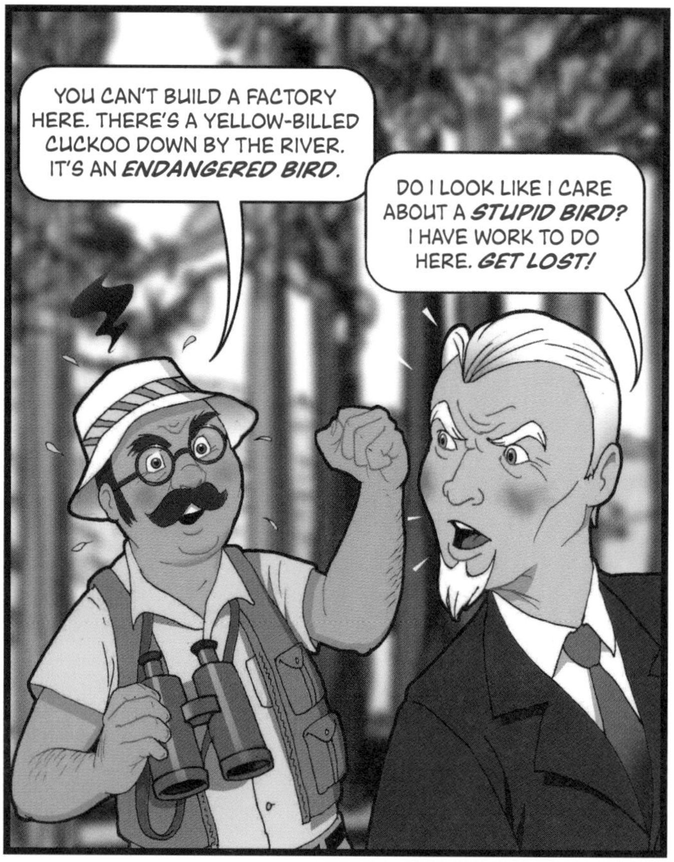
YOU CAN'T BUILD A FACTORY HERE. THERE'S A YELLOW-BILLED CUCKOO DOWN BY THE RIVER. IT'S AN ENDANGERED BIRD.
DO I LOOK LIKE I CARE ABOUT A STUPID BIRD? I HAVE WORK TO DO HERE. GET LOST!

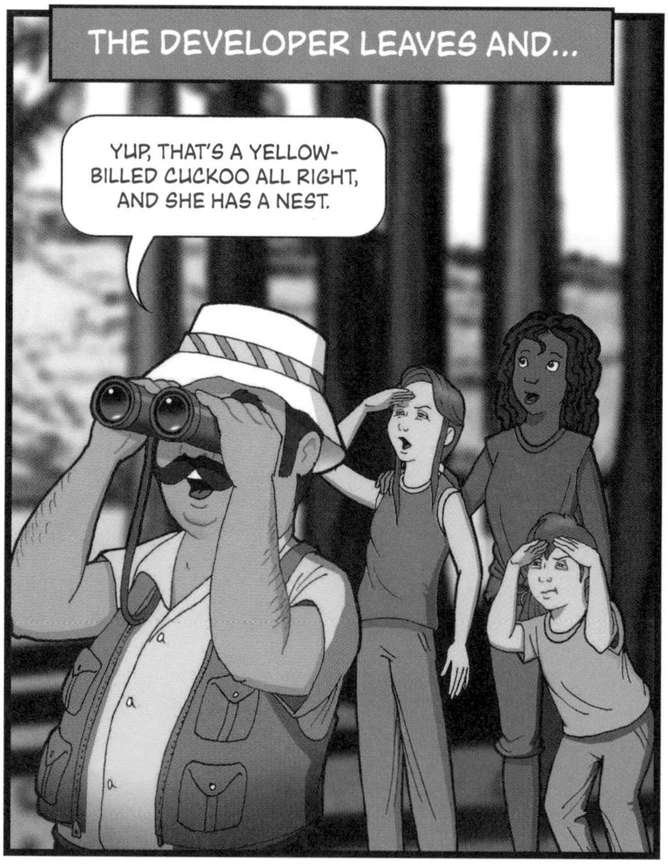
THE DEVELOPER LEAVES AND...
YUP, THAT'S A YELLOW-BILLED CUCKOO ALL RIGHT, AND SHE HAS A NEST.

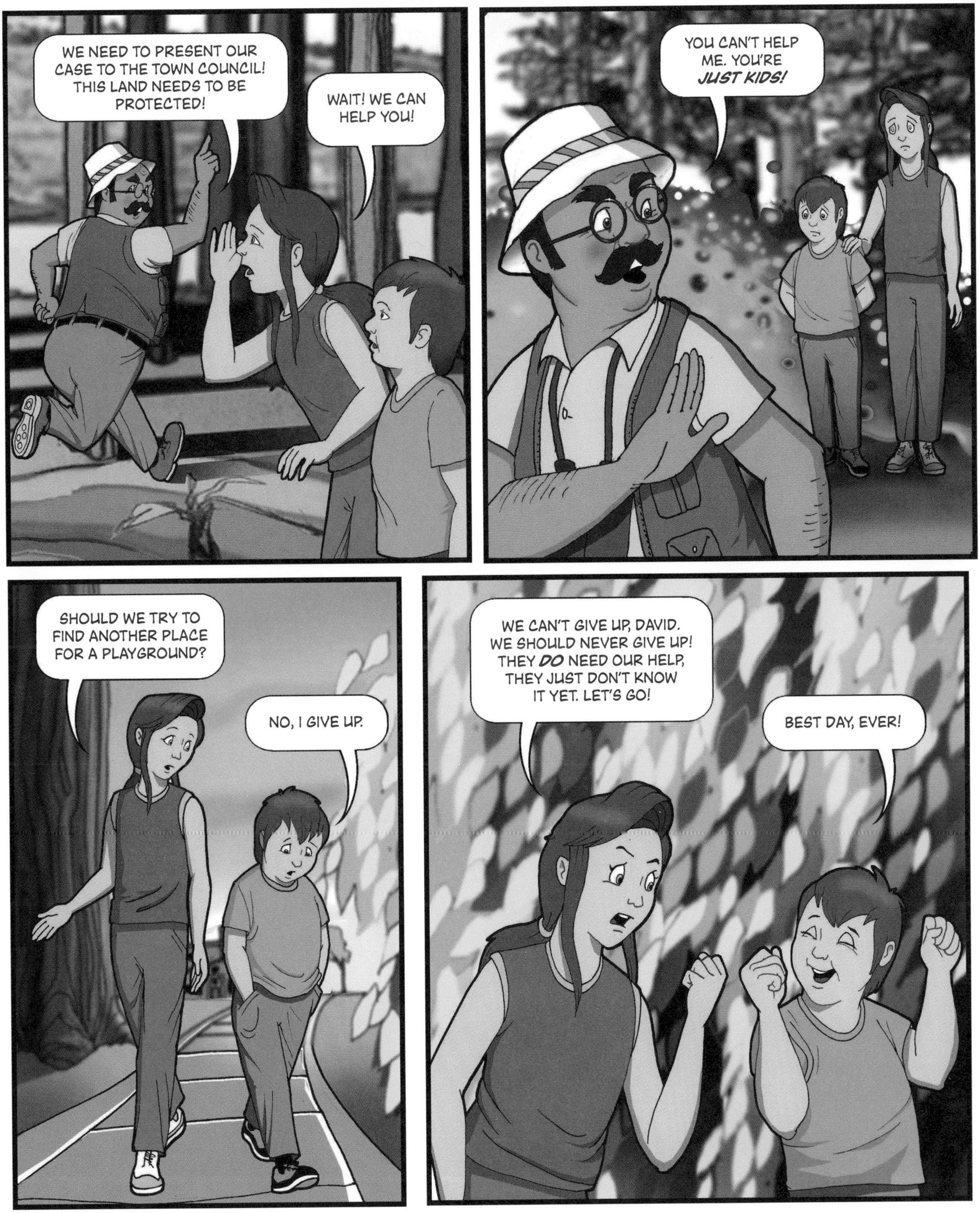
WE NEED TO PRESENT OUR CASE TO THE TOWN COUNCIL! THIS LAND NEEDS TO BE PROTECTED!
WAIT! WE CAN HELP YOU!
YOU CAN'T HELP ME. YOU'RE *JUST KIDS!*
SHOULD WE TRY TO FIND ANOTHER PLACE FOR A PLAYGROUND?
NO, I GIVE UP.
WE CAN'T GIVE UP, DAVID. WE SHOULD NEVER GIVE UP! THEY *DO* NEED OUR HELP, THEY JUST DON'T KNOW IT YET. LET'S GO!
BEST DAY, EVER!

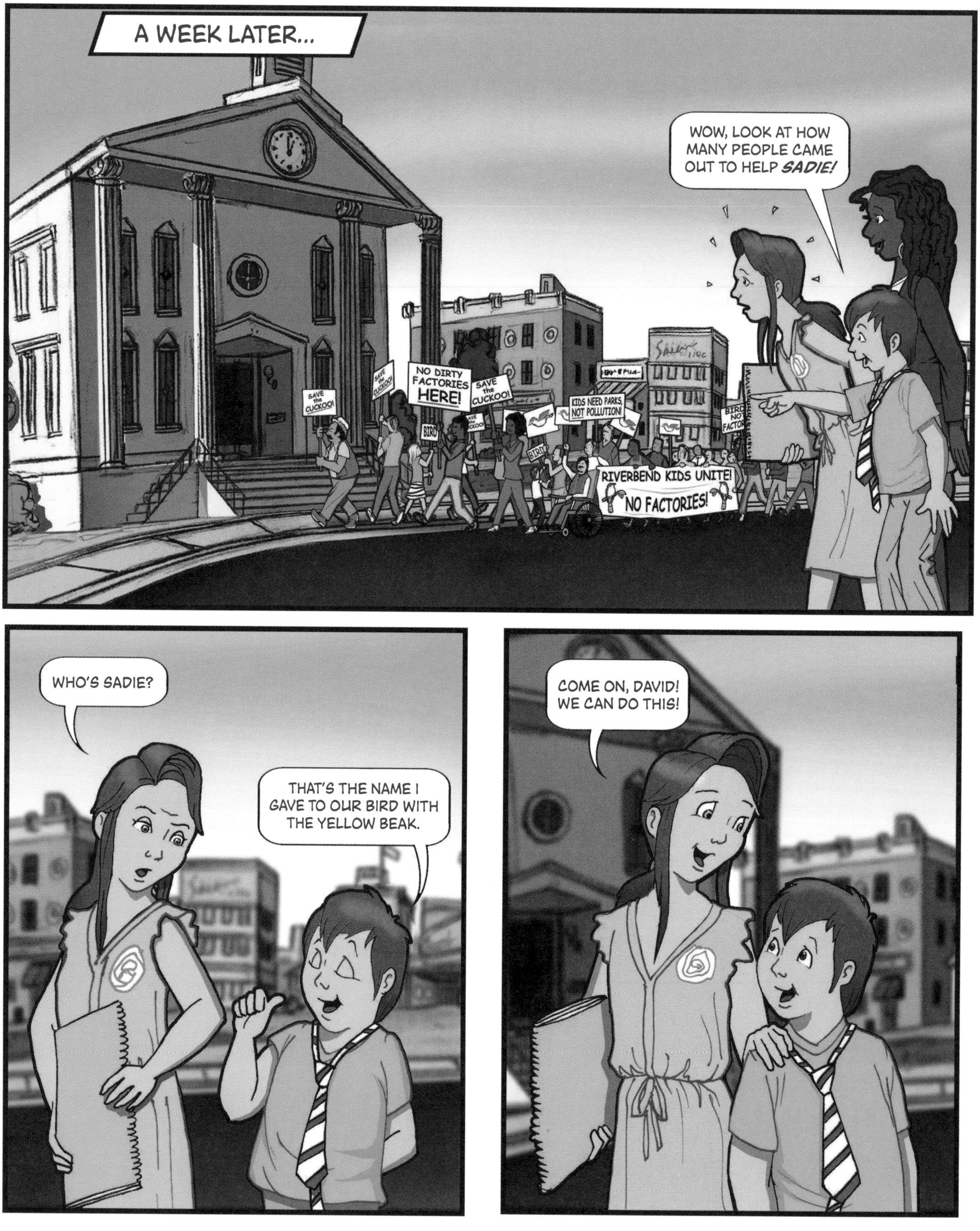
A WEEK LATER...
SAVE the CUCKOO!
SAVE the CUCKOO!
NO DIRTY FACTORIES HERE!
SAVE the CUCKOO!
KIDS NEED PARKS, NOT POLLUTION!
RIVERBEND KIDS UNITE!
NO FACTORIES!
WOW, LOOK AT HOW MANY PEOPLE CAME OUT TO HELP *SADIE!*
WHO'S SADIE?
THAT'S THE NAME I GAVE TO OUR BIRD WITH THE YELLOW BEAK.
COME ON, DAVID! WE CAN DO THIS!

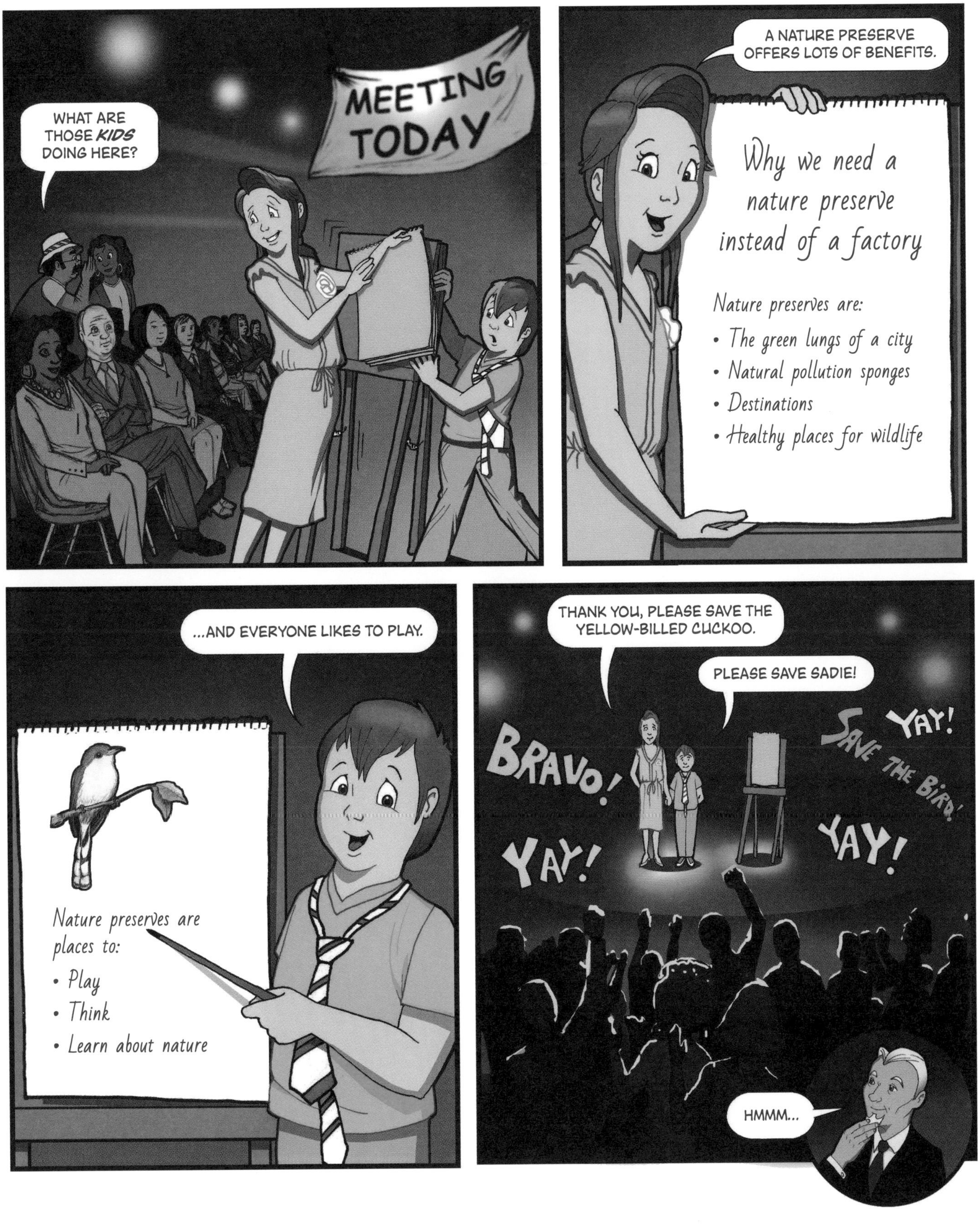
MEETING TODAY
WHAT ARE THOSE *KIDS* DOING HERE?
A NATURE PRESERVE OFFERS LOTS OF BENEFITS.
Why we need a nature preserve instead of a factory
Nature preserves are:
• The green lungs of a city
• Natural pollution sponges
• Destinations
• Healthy places for wildlife
...AND EVERYONE LIKES TO PLAY.
Nature preserves are places to:
• Play
• Think
• Learn about nature
THANK YOU, PLEASE SAVE THE YELLOW-BILLED CUCKOO.
PLEASE SAVE SADIE!
BRAVO!
YAY!
SAVE THE BIRD!
YAY!
YAY!
HMMM...

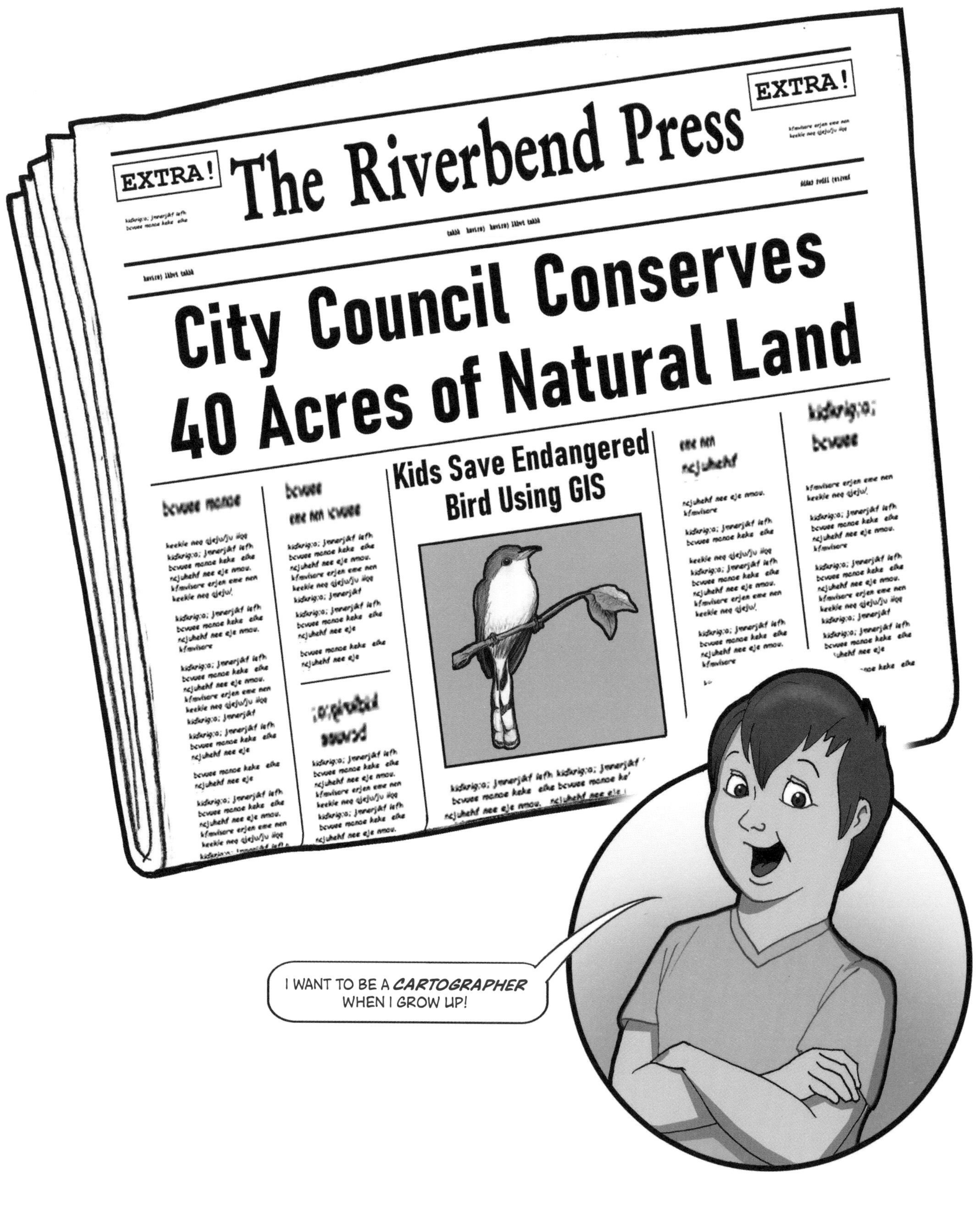
EXTRA!
The Riverbend Press
EXTRA!
City Council Conserves 40 Acres of Natural Land
Kids Save Endangered Bird Using GIS
I WANT TO BE A *CARTOGRAPHER* WHEN I GROW UP!

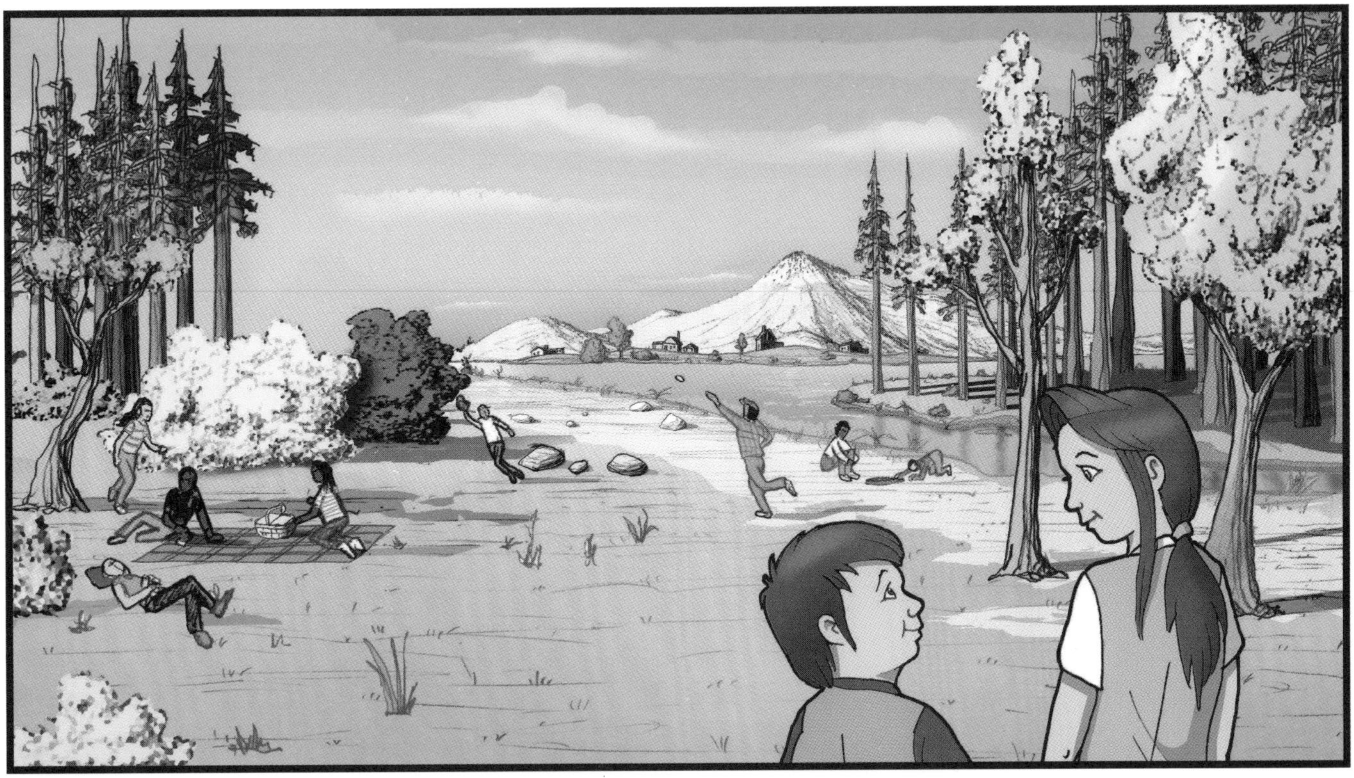

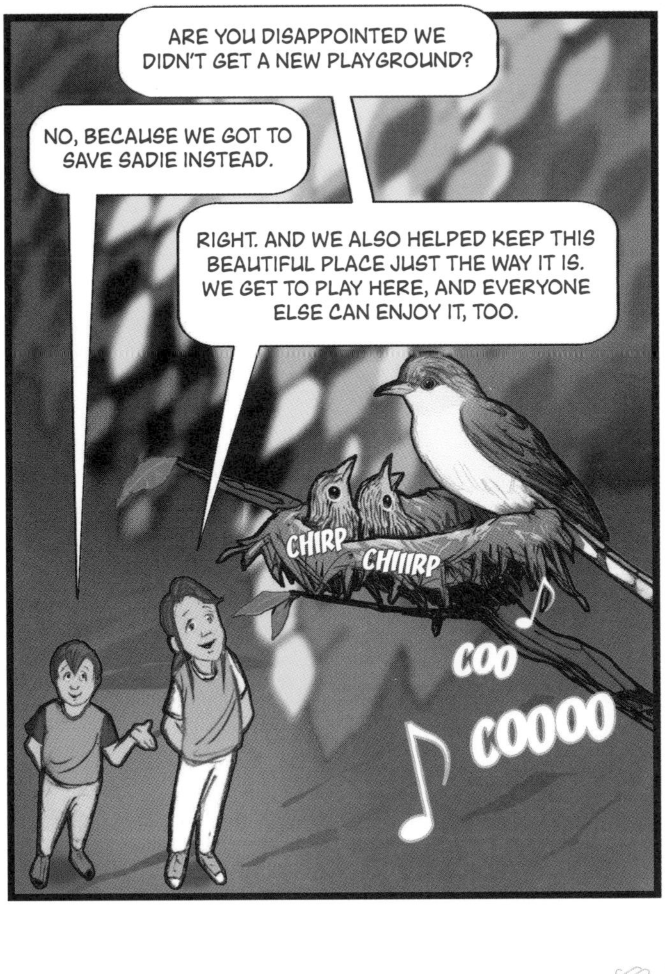
ARE YOU DISAPPOINTED WE DIDN'T GET A NEW PLAYGROUND?
NO, BECAUSE WE GOT TO SAVE SADIE INSTEAD.
RIGHT. AND WE ALSO HELPED KEEP THIS BEAUTIFUL PLACE JUST THE WAY IT IS. WE GET TO PLAY HERE, AND EVERYONE ELSE CAN ENJOY IT, TOO.
CHIRP
CHIIIRP
COO
COOOO

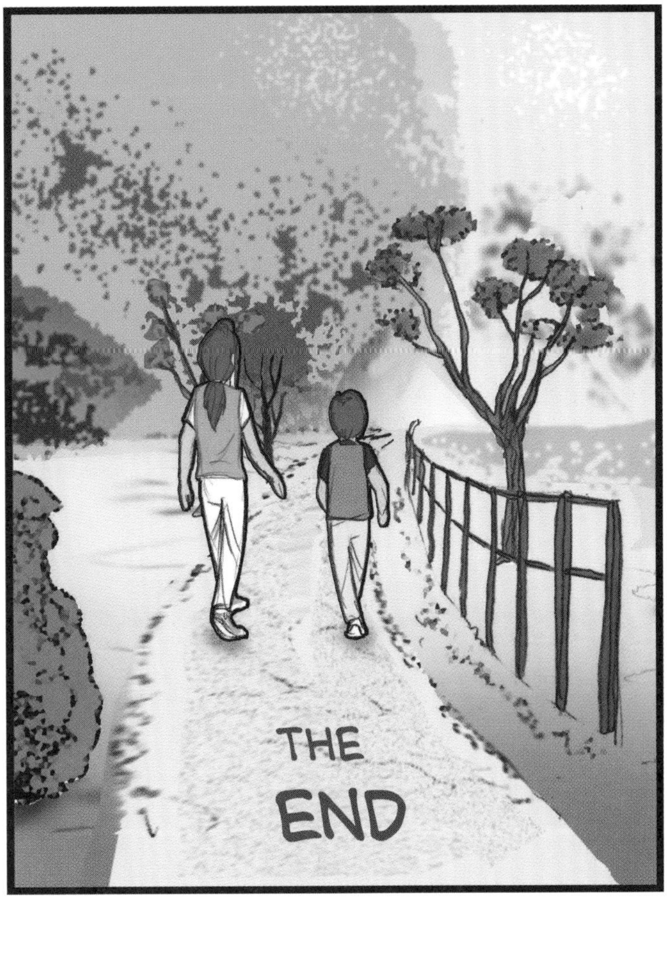
THE
END

Glossary

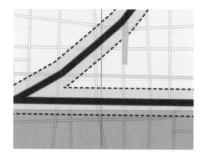

Buffer

The word **buffer** can mean an area separating things that don't belong together.

*Draw a one-mile **buffer** around the freeway so we only consider park locations that are separated from freeway traffic.*

Buffer can also mean an area around things, used to summarize what's there.

*Draw a 10-minute walk time **buffer** around the park and count the number of houses within the **buffer** area.*

Binoculars

You can hold **binoculars** up to your eyes to see farther. They contain two small telescopes that make things far away seem closer to you.

*Please pass me the **binoculars**. I think I see an eagle on the other side of the lake!*

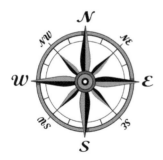

Cardinal directions

There are four **cardinal directions**: north, east, south, and west. The word *cardinal* means they are the basic or most important directions.

*The compass on a map shows the **cardinal directions**, which are usually abbreviated as N, E, S, and W.*

Cartographer

A **cartographer** is someone who creates maps on paper or by using mapping software on a computer.

*Working as a **cartographer** is a great career for someone who likes maps, spatial analysis, art, and computers.*

City council

A **city council** is a group of elected officials who help run a city. They make decisions about city projects, and they do their best to represent the interests of the city and its people.

We need to bring up our concerns about the new factory to the members of the city council.

Compass

A **compass** is a tool for finding direction. It has a magnetic needle that can spin, but because of the magnet, it always points north. Maps also have a **compass** to show which direction is north.

*Holding the **compass** in her hand, she can orient the map so both the handheld **compass** and the drawn map **compass** point north.*

Endangered species

An **endangered species** is any animal, plant, or fish that is in danger of disappearing forever. Many birds, including the yellow-billed cuckoo and the snowy owl, are at risk of becoming extinct.

*Many countries have laws to protect tigers because they are an **endangered species**. There are very few of them left on the planet.*

Flip chart

A **flip chart** is a large pad of paper on a stand. You can write on the paper, and then flip the page to see the next page.

*We'll use a **flip chart** to present our ideas to the city council.*

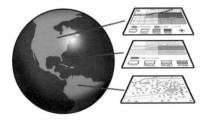

GIS

GIS stands for *geographic information systems*. **GIS** software on a computer is used to create maps and analyze spatial data.

*We'll use **GIS** to organize all our maps and data, and to help us find the best place for a new park.*

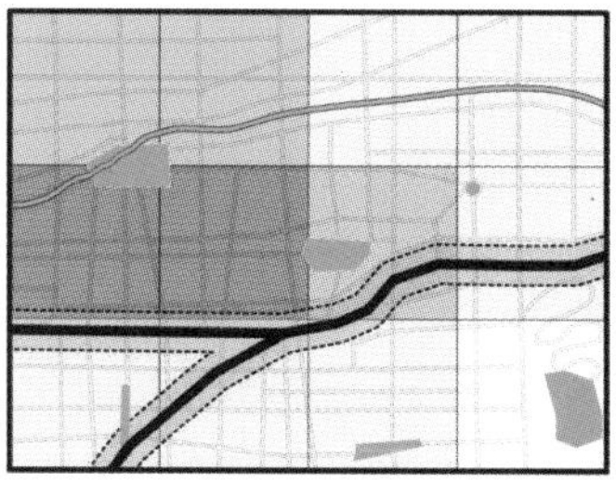

Map

A ***map*** is a drawing or representation of a place. It shows where things are and how far apart those things are from each other. Maps might show rivers, lakes, forests, buildings, or the roads in a city. Sometimes ***maps*** show things that can't be seen, such as temperatures.

*He looked at the **map** to see how much farther he needed to go.*

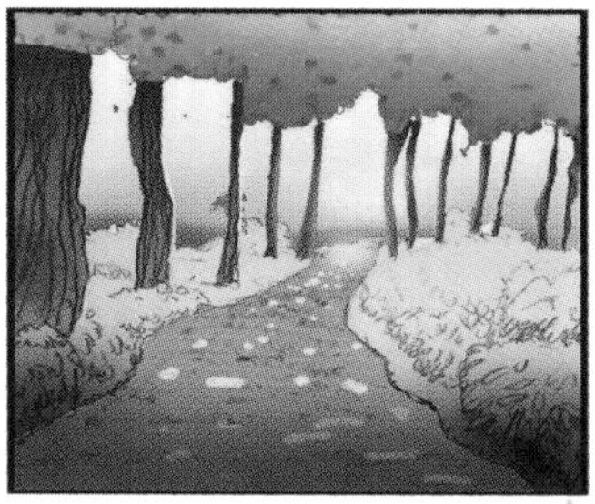

Nature preserve

A ***nature preserve*** is a protected area where plants and animals can thrive in their natural settings. Often hiking, picnicking, and research are also permitted.

*That section of public land has been set aside as a **nature preserve** where researchers can study plants and animals.*

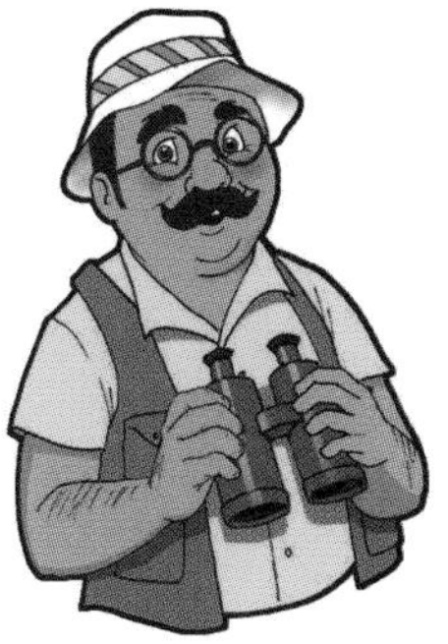

Ornithologist

An ***ornithologist*** is someone who studies birds. Their work involves surveying, recording, and reporting bird activity. ***Ornithologists*** are bird experts.

*Mr. Sanchez is an **ornithologist**. He knows all about birds.*

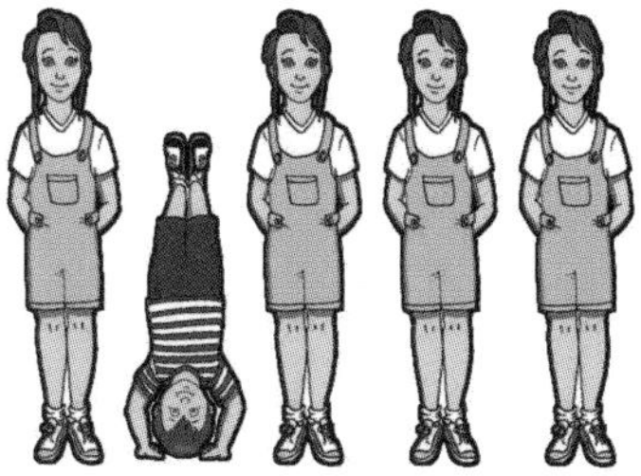

Outlier

An ***outlier*** is something that is very different or very unusual from everything around it. If a group of numbers are near 20 (21, 20, 22, 21, 23, 19), but one number is much larger (3,246), that number is an ***outlier***.

*Everyone in the marching band is wearing the same black uniform except the guy in the middle wearing a bright, flowery shirt. His shirt is an **outlier**.*

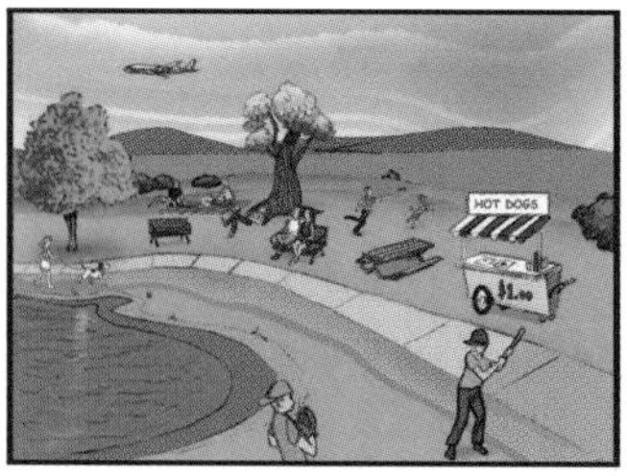
HOT DOGS

Park

A ***park*** is a large public green space with grass and trees set aside for hiking, playing, and enjoying nature.

*Let's have a picnic at the **park**!*

Spatial analysis

Someone doing **spatial analysis** looks at data (such as numbers) but also looks at locations (where those numbers are). They analyze, study, and map the numbers to understand spatial patterns and spatial relationships in the data.

*Let's do a **spatial analysis** of kids in our class to see who lives closest to the school.*

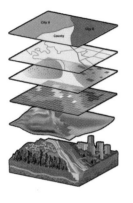

Spatial overlay

A **spatial overlay** combines layers of information for the same area to better understand the relationships among them. Usually, each layer is a map of the same area showing a different thing. If you overlay a map of roads with a map of buildings, you can see the spatial connections between the roads and the buildings.

*We'll create a **spatial overlay** of roads, houses, and open land to find the best place for a new park.*

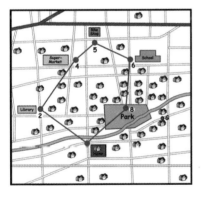

Walk time

A **walk time** map shows how far people can walk from a location to any other location within a certain amount of time. Most people can walk about ¼ mile (around 400 meters) in 5 minutes. This can be shown on a map as a 5-minute walk buffer.

*Draw a circle around the park to show how many people are within a 5-minute **walk time** of it.*

Yellow-billed cuckoo

The **yellow-billed cuckoo** is sometimes called the "rain crow" because you often hear its song before thunderstorms. Once a commonly seen bird, it is now threatened because the areas near rivers, where it likes to make its home, are being replaced by cities, dams, livestock pastures, and construction.

*Look, there's a **yellow-billed cuckoo** in the tree above the river!*

Activity Solutions

Page 5. The compass activity teaches **cardinal directions** and **map reading**. It incorporates the following spatial concepts and skills: **direction**, **orientation**, **relative spatial relationships**, and **spatial terms**. The solution is shown below.

JUNK YARD
START HERE

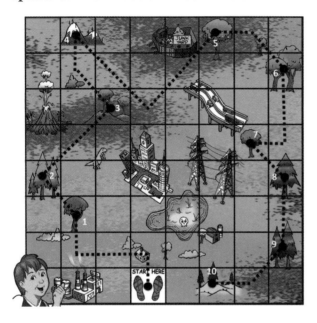

Page 7. Where is the best place for a new park? Building on the previous activity, this activity requires the reader to consider **spatial relationships** and **spatial context** to answer three questions. Answers may vary from the following.

Top. The park will have cleaner air and nicer views if it is west of the factory because the wind will keep the factory smoke to the east, away from the park.

Middle. The park will have less noise and less car exhaust farther from the freeway and closer to a quiet road.

Bottom. More people will be able to enjoy the park if it is close to where everyone lives. If the park is in the city where everyone works or far out in the country, neighborhood kids will have a harder time getting to it.

Page 10. Maps show how far away things are. To answer these questions, readers need to evaluate **spatial** and **mathematical relationships**.

Top. Count the dots from the park to the school. The dot over the middle of the school is six dots from the park, so it is about six minutes away.

Middle. Since the park where the kids are playing looks much closer to the bike shop than the store, it must be about five miles away from the bike shop.

Bottom. The letter that is most central to all three places will be closest (most accessible). Notice that the letter *B* is almost exactly in the middle of all three places. To show that *B* is closest to the park, the school, and the store, draw equidistant marks along each of the lines and count the total number of marks associated with each letter. In the diagram below, *A* (green) has 25 marks, *B* (purple) has 19 marks, and *C* (orange) has 27 marks. *B* is closest to everything, followed by *A* and then *C*.

A
B
C
Park
Store
School

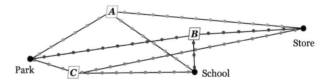

Page 12. Mark the good and bad places for a new park. This activity exercises **spatial reasoning** based on **spatial context**. The freeway, airport, mall, train station, area with electrical towers, dump, toxic area, and factory site are not appropriate for a park. Good places for a park include the forest, beach, flower field, riverside, valley, meadow, orchard, and tree-lined trail.

Page 14. Identify outliers. This activity exercises the ability to **detect differences** and notice the unexpected.

Top. David, of course!

Middle. There are three very nice parks with people playing. The playground, though, has big electrical towers near it. Playing and electrical towers don't go together. The electrical poles are the outliers.

Bottom. (1) The airplane on the left becomes a flying saucer on the right. (2) There isn't a tree behind the Frisbee-catching dog on the left, but there is a tree on the right. (3) The girl walking a dog near the lake on the left is walking a rhino on the right. (4) The sign says hot dogs on the left and hamburgers on the right. (5) The batter has a bat on the left and a tennis racket on the right.

Pages 17–19. Spatial overlay. These coloring activities demonstrate how a **spatial overlay** works. Each layer adds new information to the map, identifying the best locations for a new park. The activity builds skills in **map reading** and **data visualization**.

Page 17. Color the squares based on the number of people and the legend provided.

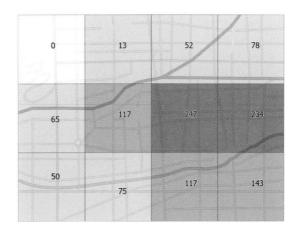

Page 18. Color the freeway black and color the buffer around the freeway gray.

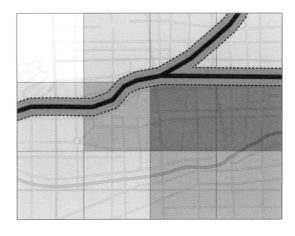

Page 19. Unsuitable park locations that have too few people, are inaccessible, or are too close to the freeway are crossed off.

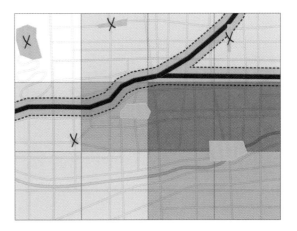

Page 20. Coloring page that includes a map.

Page 21. Connect the dots. This activity builds skills in **map reading** and **map drawing**. It teaches the concepts of **walk time distance**, **accessibility**, and **population density**.

The left buffer touches or encloses fewer housing features (about 11). The right buffer touches or encloses many more (about 28), so it has the higher population density.

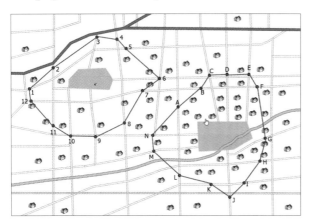

Opportunities to extend the activities in this book
Resources for parents and teachers

Kayla's projects. Forest health, homelessness, and siting a new bike shop.

- Explore fun activities for kids by the US Forest Service: **https://www.fs.fed.us/learn/kids**

- Talk about homelessness. This may help: **https://www.uwkc.org/homelessness/ talk-homelessness-with-kids**

- Discuss what makes a location good for a new bike shop. (Near what? What kind of setting? What kind of people?)

Compass direction activities

Take the children outside and notice where the sun is. Talk about how it rises in the east and sets in the west. If possible, point out landmarks to help them find north, south, east, and west.

Make a large, simple map of their school and the streets around it (use ArcGIS Online or Google Maps, for example). Mark where the school is. Have the children find their own homes on the map. Encourage conversations about which kids live close or far, and which children live near each other.

Hand out maps of the school and surrounding streets. Have the kids show their house and provide compass directions to get from their home to the school.

Landmark activities

Ask students to draw a simple map of their school from memory, and then compare it with a professionally drawn floor plan. Compare the two and identify the places where the two maps align most closely and deviate most drastically. Why might a student's memory of the layout of the school differ from the geographic reality? Which locations show up consistently across many students' maps? These common features, which have well-known locations and are at least somewhat notable, are called landmarks.

Discuss the pros and cons of giving directions using a map and compass versus verbal descriptions using landmarks. When would you use one over the other?

Organize students into small groups and instruct them to share verbal directions from the school to their house, including landmarks and street names where appropriate. At the end of the class, group the students back together and ask them to repeat the directions they were given by the others. Which students' directions were most memorable, and why?

Distance activities

Create a large number line on the floor or sidewalk and have the children use it to do addition and subtraction.

Set up three chairs. Have a couple of children stand in different locations between the three chairs. Ask onlookers to determine who is closest to all three chairs. Have them count steps from each centered child to each chair. The child with the smallest number of summed steps is the most central. Why might it be important to know which place is most central? Give examples—the school should be central to the students, the grocery store should be central to the homes, the park should be central to the children who play there, and so on.

Hand out graph paper with three x,y coordinates plotted on it and instruct the students to find the mean center of the three points. The x- and y-coordinates of the mean center are found by computing the averages of the starting points' x- and y-values, as shown in the graphic below.

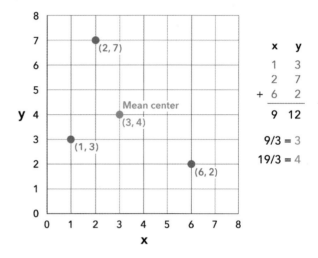

For an additional challenge, plot more than three points and instruct the students to guess where the mean center will be before calculating it. How does introducing an outlier affect the location of the mean center?

Grouping and outlier activities

Have the children answer: What does a forest look like? What does it *not* look like?

For a classroom with more than a few students, have them group themselves by height, and then by hair color. Lead them in a discussion about diversity. This resource may help: **https://extension.psu. edu/programs/betterkidcare/knowledge- areas/environment-curriculum/activities/ all-activities/we-are-different-we-are- the-same-teaching-young-children-about- diversity**

List four words and have the children identify which are similar (belong in the same group) and which one is different (the outlier). What makes the words in each set similar?

- Red, blue, table, purple
- Above, small, below, beside
- Big, green, large, small
- Playground, eyes, nose, ear
- Potato, broccoli, fork, carrot

Mapping activities

Have the children draw a map of their classroom or bedroom.

Have them sketch a map of the neighborhood where they live.

Have them design and map a new playground. They should decide if it will have swings, a baseball field, a picnic table, and so forth.

Exploring spatial careers

Students interested in careers in the spatial sciences may enjoy the STEAM at Work! book series, also from Esri Press, which showcases careers in GIS, civil engineering, landscape architecture, urban planning, and more.

Each book features a companion website with printable activities, teacher resources, and an interactive map that illustrates the usefulness of GIS to that discipline. Information on the book series and links to the companion websites can be found at **SteamAtWork.com**.

Advanced resources

Esri continues to develop more and more resources for children, parents, and teachers. If kids are excited about this book, be sure to check out these additional resources:

Mapping Hour for Parents and Teachers. This website introduces online geographic software that can be incorporated into K–12 classes or for learning at home: **https://mappinghour-k12.hub.arcgis.com**

Teach with GIS. Designed for teachers and parents with very little GIS experience, this site can be used to develop interest in GIS: **https://teach-with-gis-learngis.hub.arcgis.com**

ArcGIS Blog: Take Your Work to Kids Day, Challenge 1: Coloring In. Enthusiastic parents who work in GIS have developed these resources: **https://www.esri.com/arcgis-blog /products/arcgis-pro/education/take-your-work-to-kids-day-challenge-1-coloring-in**

GIS for Kids: An Introduction to GIS for 4th and 5th Graders. This story map is meant for kids in grades 4 and 5: **https://storymaps.arcgis.com/stories/854 cad1bba294608b79fe35b54b08a87**

GIS Day Resources for Event Hosts. Learn more about GIS Day, which is celebrated every year in the fall. This link is for 2020; scroll down to find resources for children: **https://www.gisday.com/en-us/resources**

Keep checking around the web for more resources to help your kids and students learn.